Slow Urban Planning

jovis

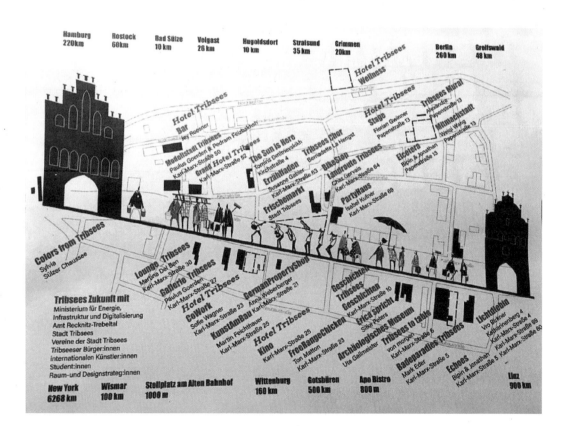

Hamburg 220km · Rostock 60km · Bad Sülze 10 km · Wolgast 26 km · Hugoldsdorf 10 km · Stralsund 35 km · Grimmen 20km · Berlin 260 km · Greifswald 48 km

Hotel Tribsees Wellness

Hotel Tribsees Bar
Joey Roedder

Hotel Tribsees Stage
Florian Gwinner Papenstraße T3

Tribsees Mural
Mirandola Papenstraße 13

Modellstadt Tribsees
Paulus Goerden & Pedram Feizbakhsh
Karl-Marx-Straße 50

Mitmachstadt
Wendi Wang Papenstraße 13

The Sun Is Here
Tomris Dmirmeyekliah Kirchstraße 4

Tribsees Chor
Bernadette La Hengst

Grand Hotel Tribsees
Karl-Marx-Straße 52

Eicotera
Bipin & Jonathan Papenstraße 13

Erzählladen
Susanne Gabler
Karl-Marx-Straße 53

Bikeshop

Landroute Tribsees
Chaz Gervais
Karl-Marx-Straße 64

Frischemarkt
Stadt Tribsees

PartyHaus
Isobel Kufner
Karl-Marx-Straße 66

Colors from Tribsees
Sylvia
Sülzer Chaussee

Lounge Tribsees
Marcria Del Ben
Karl-Marx-Straße 30

Gallerie Tribsees
Paulus Goerden
Karl-Marx-Straße 27

German Property Shop
Anna Weberberger Karl-Marx-Straße 21

Geschichten Tribsees Geschichten
Karl-Marx-Straße 10

Lichtatelier
Vro Blöfner
Kellnerinenberg 4
Karl-Marx-Straße 69

Tribsees Zukunft mit
Ministerium für Energie, Infrastruktur und Digitalisierung
Amt Recknitz-Trebeltal
Stadt Tribsees
Vereine der Stadt Tribsees
Tribseeser Bürger:innen
internationalen Künstler:innen
Student:innen
Raum-und Designstrateg:innen

CoWork
Sofie Wagner
Karl-Marx-Straße 23

Hotel Tribsees

KunstAmBau
Martin Feichtlhauer
Karl-Marx-Straße 25

Hotel Tribsees
Karl-Marx-Straße 25

Kino

FreeRangeChicken
Ton Matton
Karl-Marx-Straße 23

Erica spricht
Silke Peters

Archäologisches Museum
Uta Gellmeister

Tribsees to table
von morgen
Karl-Marx-Straße 6

Badeparadies Tribsees
Mark Eder
Karl-Marx-Straße 5

Echoes
Bipin & Jonathan
Karl-Marx-Straße 5

New York 6268 km · Wismar 100 km · Stellplatz am Alten Bahnhof 1000 m · Wittenburg 160 km · Gotsbüren 500 km · Apo Bistro 800 m · Linz 900 km

The Future of Tribsees

Slow Urban Planning Ton Matton

jovis

Table of Contents

Irrepressible Christian Pegel

Dear Tribseeers, Friends of the Town on the Trebel, Visitors, and Readers: "Making Tribsees's Future"—Professor Ton Matton's students had nothing less in mind when they came to Vorpommern from Linz, Austria, for a semester project in autumn 2020. Joined by a team of local artists, their ambitions were high; their ideas ranged from the humorous to the whimsical; and their desire to dare to do something new was irrepressible. I have fond memories of my visits to Tribsees and the refreshing conversations there: whether it was about light installations, musical designs, photographic works, or gastronomic innovations; you could always sense the underlying desire to help a community gain additional self-confidence through their imaginative concepts. The young people who set out to give Tribsees new and sometimes somewhat different ideas for living were neither art students nor urban planners. In the course of their space&designStrategies studies, they explored ways of developing rural places. I was fascinated by their unconventional approaches. What we often perceived as problems—vacant houses, patchy infrastructure, young people moving away—they just saw as opportunities.

I was very pleased to see how enthusiastic people in Vorpommern can be—how a city in our region was seen in a new light thanks to the

creativity of "strangers," and how hidden energies and talents were uncovered and pooled together. Whether it was regional artists, children's groups, or clubs that collaborated to get something going—a new perspective on something that already existed was always the result.

The state government was very happy to support this project. As Minister of the Interior and Municipal Affairs, who is also responsible for local government oversight, I can hardly imagine anything better than these kinds of creative processes that bring dedicated local people together with the goal of making their town or village more attractive. This benefits not only their visitors, but first and foremost the locals themselves— those who make their home there. I am sure that the end of this one-year project does not mean the end of

the exploration of its themes. I hope that both the artists and the young Austrians benefited in their studies of what makes a small northern German community tick. I also hope that the people of Tribsees will maintain the momentum generated this year as well as the unusual approaches to urban development problems, and that they will continue in the spirit of the project's title.

Warmly,
Christian Pegel

Minister of the Interior, Building, and Digitalization Mecklenburg-Vorpommern

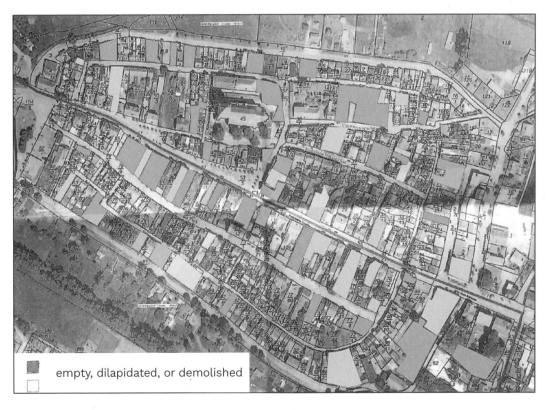

empty, dilapidated, or demolished

Karl-Marx-Straße

Seeing the Future Ton Matton & Sofie Wagner

During our first meeting, we explained our plan to occupy and experiment with the vacant buildings. Together with artists and students, we wanted to involve the local residents and inspire them to take the future of Tribsees into their own hands! There was homemade pumpkin soup and bread, followed by a tour of the more-than-seventy vacant buildings. Many ideas came up in the process: Tribsees as a retirement town, an energy-neutral town, an artisanal town, a free-range chicken town, a climate-resilient town, the first town to be sent to the moon by Elon Musk, and more. Many ideas had a certain

romanticism in common, a longing for the rusticity of the past—when life was a bit slower—while still being aware of future developments. And the old saying, "In Mecklenburg-Vorpommern, everything happens fifty years later," was heard in the evening. Well then, I thought to myself, what Tribsees needs is a kind of easy-going, a slow urban planning.

Karl-Marx-Straße

Dancing the Tango Ute Gallmeister & Tanja Blankenburg

For hours the musicians of Muzet Royal played their tango music in front of the former department store. Several tango clubs from Schwerin and Greifswald exploited the ambience to perform their tango dances, and even some Tribsees residents danced in the magical sunset.

Banana Tree

... in which a retired mayor, we'll call him BZ, tells the story of how revolutionary easy-going urban planning was introduced about twenty-five years ago.

We see BZ standing in a simple cottage on Ostmauerstraße in Tribsees, with a banana grove in the background and ring-necked parakeets flying above.

BZ: At the time, we were looking for possible future scenarios for Tribsees. A group of artists and students came to play around with the empty houses of the town. Pretty crazy, to be honest. But that's exactly what Tribsees needed to get out of the dead end that the town was stuck in. Through improvised urban living, they introduced a performative urbanism that pushed the limits of what was deemed possible, to explore innovative spatial solutions.

L: Innovative spatial solutions?

BZ: Yes, that is, concepts that are neither conventional nor obvious. As politicians, we noticed that the developments of the past decades had not helped Tribsees to develop in a positive way—as was true for many other small towns in the state of Mecklenburg-Vorpommern. All the investments in new roads and new sewage systems were apparently not enough. There were still many vacant properties, and not enough people moving in. And with all

Ostmauerstraße

those crumbling houses in the town center … things kept going downhill. Through their project, the artists wanted to obscure the negative history and replace it with positive approaches. Then, if someone was interested in moving to Tribsees, they could talk about their positive experiences—"Here we did our ironing together last week, there we danced the tango in the street …"—instead of always repeating the same negative stories about empty buildings. It was an exciting and bold process for everyone involved, both for the minister and for those of us from the municipal administration, as well as for local associations, the residents and, of course, for the artists and students involved. And I have to say it was worth it, a town that clearly had been battered gained new ideas and with them also a new future.

There were more and more owners who wanted to do something about vacant properties, and in general residents developed a greater sense of responsibility for their own town. On the one hand, this was because these zany artistic projects made them feel a little more self-confident—the students and artists were genuinely curious and didn't arrive with patronizing, big city ideas. On the other, it was also because more and more young families were moving back to Tribsees, having experienced the big city and made the conscious decision to live in the countryside. This strengthened the sense that each person can and must do something for their own town in order to bring about change.

Karl-Marx-Straße

Tribsees Camping Motorsports Club

Despite the name, the Motorsports
Club has nothing to do with
motorcycles. In the Tribsees club,
about a hundred members get together
in their campers at a wide variety of
campsites across Europe. This time
they met on Karl-Marx-Straße, which
was transformed into a campsite for a
day. Dressed in summery outfits, the
members met again after two years of
the coronavirus hiatus, equipped with
camping tables and stools on hand,
plenty of coffee, homemade cake, and
even some camper vans. Naturally,
the requisite bottles of liquor had also
been packed. And as soon as the NDR
television team appeared, they sang a
song together. Just the way romantic
life in the country is supposed to be!

System Error

"Make no little plans, they have no magic to stir men's blood and probably themselves will not be realized. Make big plans."[1]

This text begins with this well-known citation from Daniel Burnham, because Tribsees has a potential that it deserves to achieve. This small Pomeranian town on the Trebel River has a centuries-old town center structure that has been almost completely preserved. Encircled by city walls and ramparts, with two beautiful towers standing at either side of the 400-meter-long Karl-Marx-Straße, Tribsees has a fabled ensemble of streets, alleys, and *Quebbe* accentuated with splendid buildings.[2] Unfortunately, however, about thirty percent of its buildings are vacant. Of about 250 houses in the town center, more than seventy are dilapidated and decaying, while some have already been demolished and their rubble disposed of. We have to ask: how can it be that a town in which urban development funds[3] were invested following reunification has become so run-down? Is it just coincidence and bad luck? Have the policies failed? Is the town in the wrong geographical location? Is it a capitalist system error?

The fact is that vacancy in Tribsees is a big problem. You can become discouraged by it when confronted with it every day. But at the same time, it is possible to sense a huge opportunity, as the lack of space in big cities is leading to high rents and (for many) unaffordable housing prices. The German Federal Minister for Housing, Urban Development, and Building, Klara Geywitz, explained in an interview in the magazine *Der Spiegel* that she wants to create incentives so that more young families buy and renovate old houses.[4] A growing desire to live in the countryside, in villages and small towns, is palpable; it can be felt in Tribsees, with interest in vacant lots

1   Daniel Burnham, quoted from: Daniel Burnham, Edward H. Bennett, *Plan of Chicago*, Chicago: The Commercial Club, 1909.
2   "Quebbe" is an archaic German word unique to this area that is used for some street names in Tribsees. See: Dieter Greve, "Flurnamen in Mecklenburg-Vorpommern mit einem Lexikon der Flurnamenelemente (Flurnamen von A bis Z)," Schwerin: 2016, p. 101; https://stiftung-mecklenburg.de/wp-content/uploads/2017/02/Dieter_Greve_Flurnamen_von_A_bis_Z.pdf (accessed March 6, 2023).

3   Read more at www.staedtebaufoerderung.info (accessed March 6, 2023).
4   Urban planning is about resilience again: Interview by Sebastian Fischer, Henning Jauernig, and Christian Teevs with Klara Geywitz: "Bauministerin Geywitz über Sanierungspflicht von Immobilien. 'Es wird nicht ohne Ordnungsrecht gehen, wenn wir die Klimaziele erreichen wollen'" (March 26, 2022), *Der Spiegel,* no. 13, pp. 30–33.

increasing. However, in these neoliberal times, this leads to the next problem, that of gentrification and investing for the sake of investing. Fast money always manages to find its way and is invested, not to bring the town back to life, but to make a profit. While those investments—intended to generate income either through a quick sale or by housing tourists—can yield a few renovated facades, the town and its residents have little to gain from them, as there is hardly any tax revenue, there are hardly any new neighbors who participate in social life.

Abandoned Houses

Tribsees' active municipal administration is aware of this problem, and with the backing of the Ministry of Housing and Urban Development, is trying to steer this trend in a different direction to revitalize the small town. That is no easy task with so many vacant properties and unresolved or complex ownership issues. It is almost impossible to get a group of heirs with twenty-three grandchildren to sit down at the same table, to find unknown owners abroad, to clarify the ownership rights for an abandoned house, or to convince current owners to renovate their dilapidated house rather than leaving it as is in the hope of getting an even better sale price. It is clear that the bank will not invest in such renovations. After all, the bank's goal is to generate profits with as little risk as possible; a small town with seventy

derelict houses is not exactly ideal. At least the phrase often heard in the beginning—"The mayor does nothing for our broken town"—has now changed to "The mayor can't do all that much for our broken town." Even this small change in perspective brings with it a little more respect and fosters a sense of community, a shared energy, that helps the municipal administration to be even more committed to shaping the town's future.

Squatting

To better understand this small town and the processes that take place there, we—a handful of artists and students— moved to Tribsees. We occupied a run-down fish store and set up an office with co-working and co-living spaces. From there, we got to know the people of Tribsees. Step by step, we occupied more and more space, squatting in and experimenting with vacant houses and dilapidated buildings, and getting to know even more people. When we made a very similar proposal fifteen years ago in Wittenburg, where we wanted to occupy vacant houses in order to revitalize them together with the community, this was not exactly welcomed by the German Federal Ministry for Economic Affairs. They reacted as if our proposal had nothing whatsoever to do with urban planning. After I explained, as a professor, that this is exactly what I considered to be urban planning, we at least received the commission for what subsequently developed into Great Potemkin Street in Wittenburg.[5]

At the opening of Tribsees Centennial 2021, the official assessment of our approach was entirely different. In his speech, Minister Christian Pegel emphasized that it was actually not a bad idea to occupy (more or less) abandoned houses. If an owner came forward in response to the occupation, a discussion could finally take place; if not, the residents could take possession of the house and make use of it. You could call this a desperate approach. After all, it is bound up with the realization that previous urban planning efforts in Tribsees had not functioned very well. I, however, am more inclined to think of it as courageous. Courageous in that the ministry, the minister, is aware of the challenges that are common in small towns. And furthermore, it is becoming clear that the regulations we have been following do not necessarily lead to beneficial developments in small towns like Tribsees. It is becoming apparent that alternative strategies need to be developed.

Social Revitalization and Reanimation

What might new strategies for urban planning look like? It is important that the stories and events of the past are not forgotten but instead are overlaid with new experiences to open up new possibilities. In other words, what could the model of future potentials for living in the countryside look like? How might small towns and villages be socially reanimated and revitalized? Who is the target group? What strategies, what kinds of utopias could be realized?

We could not offer Tribsees guaranteed success, as we made clear right from the start. But we were able to point to projects we carried out in Wittenburg (2012) and Gottsbüren (2016),[6] both of which were in better positions after the projects were completed. We had evolved a useful dialog and developed more mutual respect among those involved. Some of the areas' vacant and dilapidated houses were even renovated or sold.

However, even these kinds of projects are unable to stop rural exodus.

Still, individual success stories have emerged that put country life in a new light, making it look attractive for the people who have always lived there and for those who have an yearning for country life but have not yet dared to move there. So, we searched for future possibilities for Tribsees—and we made big plans.

---

5   More on the project: http://www.grosse-potemkinsche-strasse.de/ (accessed March 6, 2023).

6   More on these projects: Ton Matton, ed., *Dorf machen: Improvisationen zur sozialen Wiederbelebung*, Berlin: jovis, 2017.

Tribsees Centenniale
Beginning in October 2020, we
implemented our projects in Tribsees
and finally showed them in the context
of an exhibition, the *Tribsees Centenniale*,
in summer 2021. Our quest for slow
urban planning, for easy-going urban
planning, emerged from the experience
thus gained. This does not mean
listless urban planning without vigor.
We wanted to take advantage of the
positive associations with the word
"easy-going" that small town life has
given us: relaxation, leisureliness, and
pragmatism. Even then, it still took a
lot of energy to think beyond capitalist
consumption and comfort modes
in order to develop a heterotopian
future model for Tribsees. This
resulted in fictional conversations
with townspeople, stakeholders, and
their heirs for a documentary film—
which we still want to shoot. Not
all possibilities mentioned here are
desirable, not all are probable; they are,
as I said, fictitious. This also means any
similarities to people you may know are
purely coincidental.

Karl-Marx-Straße

Umbrella Survey MattonOffice

Can everyone hear me? Good, I have some questions. If you want to answer "yes," then open your umbrella, if "no," then keep your umbrella closed. If it's raining, all questions may be answered with a "yes"!

The goal is to think further, beyond obvious things, because we already know what they are! Of course, everyone wants a restaurant. But who will promise to go out to eat in this restaurant? Who will go even if the food doesn't taste good? Or if it is too expensive? Who wants a kebab joint, food for 3.50 euros (it already exists, at Apo!)? Who prefers a gourmet restaurant with a star-rated menu for thirty-five euros? Who would like a library? Who would also like to borrow books there? Who likes the darkness in Tribsees? Who likes the moon? Who has been on the moon? Who would like to go to the moon? Who would relocate to Tribsees as the first city on the moon? Who likes eggs? Who has chickens? Who lacks space for chickens? Who thinks I'm asking the wrong questions? Who can knit socks? Who can repair shoes? Who has a sewing machine? Who wants a shoe repair shop? Who wants a dressmaker's shop? Who likes the climate in Tribsees? Has it ever been snowed in? Who likes climate change? Who is a millionaire or wants to be one? Who thinks they are poor? Who has no apartment? Who is hungry? Who would like Tribsees to be an outlet store?

Who would like to shop in this outlet, or work there? As a manager? As a salesperson? As a cleaner? Or as parking attendants for the 1,000 cars that are to be parked there in front of the tower? Who would like to be paid minimum wage for these jobs? Who would like an ice cream parlor in Tribsees? Who would like a cow? Who can make cheese? Who can make ice cream? Who wants to eat fresh croissants? Who would like to bake croissants? Who wants a coffee? Me too, the booster club there has some, bring one for me, with milk and without sugar, please! Who likes cake? They have that there, too!

It is clear that you have many desires, but it takes a lot of commitment and energy to fulfill them. So, who wants to contribute to the future of Tribsees? Please leave us a postcard with your wishes and contact details and we will get back to you!

Karl-Marx-Straße 80

Light Thief Vro Birkner

With her homemade camera obscura, Vro photographed some of the vacant buildings in Tribsees. In the process, the camera captured views from the buildings onto the town.

Karl-Marx-Straße 21

Department Store morgen.

The former department store was transformed by the Hamburg artist group morgen. together with local cooks and the filmmakers Hirn und Wanst. With incredible energy and the support of many people from Tribsees, the department store was occupied, cleaned up, and refurbished using construction waste. Several weeks of work resulted in three culinary events with a range of food from the region and beyond.

TRIBSEES TO TABLE

Karl-Marx-Straße 6
morgen. & Hirn und Wanst
Text: Martha Starke & Marco Antonio Reyes Loredo

Culinary Urban Development or: How Do We Cook Up a New Town?!

Tribsees is bitterly cold in winter, heart-warmingly beautiful in summer, and always rich in stories and history. But how does the metropolis on the Trebel River taste? And what will its future be like? Big questions. We started with very small ones, put to Ton Matton:

"Where can we go for a meal here in town?"
"Restaurant? There is none."
"Café?"
"There isn't one of those either."
"Pub?"
"Not even that."

And since we were not allowed to nibble on the exhibits at the local potato museum either, our contribution to the overall project "Making Tribsees's Future" was born out of our own experiences. After having a home-cooked meal in the local history society's kitchenette, we resolved to challenge this small town's apparent deficits through the bounties of the surrounding countryside and the skills of its inhabitants. We wanted to create a third-millennium, zero-waste restaurant that would rise from the ruins of the town and face the future—to open the place, its surrounding countryside, and even more distant regions so that they may benefit one another and celebrate together.

The ingredients for this were an empty department store, people brimming with skills and knowledge, plus everybody's hunger for friendship, conversation, and really good food. The place for it was the best building in town: the Cooperative Department Store at Karl-Marx-Straße 6, a building with palpable grandeur from the last century, date of closure and owners unknown. For us it was immediately clear—here is the spot where everything is possible! We asked the Trebel Pottery brigade, the local school, and, in fact, the whole town to help us. The prospect of having a restaurant again, a place that creates community, was well received—in Tribsees, Hamburg, and even in Bad Sülze!

It was just too bad that we didn't have the keys to the department store, or a kitchen, chairs, or tables. But we had an idea and the ambition to design a space together with the residents that could be more than simply beautiful and functional, more of a social sculpture in the sense of Beuys, less of Rach, the Restaurant Tester. And wouldn't there also be some local producers with whom we could transform the countryside into an edible landscape?

Questions upon questions. Just as it always is when culinary artists and innovative designers get down to work. The challenge was clear. The goal was somewhere on the horizon. But how could we get there?

← An inviting installation in the department store window by artist Simone Karl.

THE COUNTRYSIDE IS NOT A LANDSCAPE, THE COUNTRYSIDE IS A WAY OF THINKING.

01

01 The finest building in town: the former Konsum department store has been empty for decades. 02 How does the future taste on the Trebel? Through communal eating and drinking, we are able to enliven the area in front of the department store and stimulate conversation with the people of Tribsees.

02

RISEN FROM THE RU/NS
OF THE CITY AND
MOVING TOWARD THE
FUTURE.

Urban practice. Rural practice?

We live and operate in Hamburg. A small town like Tribsees challenges our usual methods and encourages us to question ourselves. However, to be honest, we were primarily raised in small towns or are "from the village." Our first experiences in big cities and metropolises came when became of age and received our higher education. The Tribsees to Table (T2T) experiment was therefore also a journey into our own personal histories.

In an era of simultaneity and individuality, we can become anything, and indeed already have. And so, our roles change from designer and teacher to innovator and host in a fraction of a second. For several years now, "urban practice" has stood for the creative license to make use of a wide range of disciplines, that operate as actors in cities, to transform them through their respective strategies. We are only too happy to use this terminology. But how do we justify and explain our actions here, in rural areas? Is there even such a thing as a genuine "rural practice"? And if so, what distinguishes it? We would like to clarify these questions in the following discussion, while illustrating selected approaches, formats, and objectives from our perspective.

The Gold of Tribsees

Tribsees can do pottery; that became immediately clear to us during the first public walk in 2020. The amiable senior citizen Hilde Zinke creates cups, blue frogs, and whatever else the Tribsees woman of the world needs, during her spare time at the non-profit Trebel Pottery. She immediately convinced us that she lacks neither vision nor commitment. Associations like the Trebel Pottery form the backbone of rural civil society. In small towns, the average resident belongs to twice as many associations as those in big cities. With an accomplice like Hilde, we were statistically

assured of broad access to our field of operation.

Following the example of the Granby Workshop (London), we potted together with her and her clubmates, using the bricks from crumbling houses to make tiles for the department store interior, for rubble as a resource was available by the house-load. And there was no lack of potential participants. Since each target group required a particular approach, we devised different media strategies, promotional methods, and workshop formats. A targeted press campaign and traditional mailings were the key to our success with nonaffiliated participants, whereas the experts from the pottery encouraged one another directly. In order to give something back to them as well, we invited the ceramic artist Julia Kaiser (Hamburg) to assist and direct for several days. In this way, the neighbors, local schoolchildren, and experienced potters from the association were all able to enjoy the experience in equal measure.

Over two project days with the fifth-grade classes from the Recknitz-Trebeltal elementary school, we not only potted according to the slogan "Only tiling is more beautiful," but also set out on a rally through the town so we could talk to the next generation about the future of Tribsees. How do the young people of today imagine the restaurant of tomorrow? And what kind of food do they think will be served there? We then wove the children's visions and favorite dishes into the final zero-waste restaurant plan.

In search of the hidden potential in seemingly obvious shortcomings, the idea of tile led us to our goal. Condensed to fifteen-by-fifteen centimeters, it allowed everyone to grasp the concept of T2T with their own hands. The creation process behind it also symbolizes the participatory method. We were not able to accomplish the task by ourselves, nor did we want to define it on our own. Only in reciprocal negotiations with the place, its materiality, and its residents did we achieve the acceptance and coherence that we were hoping for, and that the project needed. It is only when we enable the people of Tribsees to follow and shape the process transparently and actively that there is a possibility that something will remain, even after we are long gone.

From Department Store to Restaurant
Another obvious resource in Tribsees is the vacant properties. In the historic town center alone, more than seventy buildings stand vacant, and even more plots of land, disguised as meadows and open spaces, mask the decline of the once vibrant center. The reasons for this state of affairs are historically embedded, systemic, and on top of that, homegrown. But what approaches might be used to halt and even reverse this creeping decline? Again, there was no single answer, but we did choose a concrete approach.
For us, Karl-Marx-Staße 6 reflected the various facets of the existing problems, and in fact solutions shone through its grimy store windows. In addition to the valuable building fabric, we also recognized the potential here for a place with a built-in sense of community. Whether in the city or in the country, spaces that create a sense of community are not something that residents can take for granted in our society. What does seem normal, however, is that land is to generate monetary value, with the aim of continuously increasing it.

If, in addition to activist ideas originating from below, the assent of politicians and administrators is also forthcoming, then there is an opportunity for some unique collaborations with unexpected power. Here in Tribsees, a lot of good ideas would have been impossible without the clarity and understanding shown by the mayor, Bernhard

Zieris, and Christian Pegel, the Minister for Interior, Building, and Digitalization in the state of Mecklenburg-Vorpommern. Often, unclear ownership, lack of determination, and failure to exploit the legal framework stand in the way of development in this region.

In his opening speech on June 24, 2021, Pegel surprised everyone with his unequivocal attitude toward owners who do not fulfill their duty of care or are not even contactable. If the buildings that define the townscape are deliberately left to decay, expropriation should ultimately be an option. If these same buildings are opened to the community, only positive effects will result. The place will be upgraded and put to use, and the building fabric will perhaps even be preserved in some cases. And if the owners become aware of this and come forward, contact and possibly even dialog will occur, which seemed impossible before.

In our case, the "unreachable" owner was popularly known only as "the Swiss character." Apart from this specific nationality, there were only ambiguities and rumors. However, these were not in short supply. But we were also amazed by the dwindling collective memory. For example, dates given for when the department store closed varied not by months, but by decades. So, in addition to the building fabric, memory also crumbles as a result of dereliction.

In material terms, however, we dedicated ourselves precisely to this past and went on a treasure hunt in the building. What for others was just junk or old scrap metal became for us the raw material for a new design. "Urban mining" is the name of a movement that focuses on sustainability and life cycles. Old shelves became tables, lampshades from the time before the fall of the Berlin Wall that had never been unpacked became wall decorations, and seemingly random odds and ends were transformed into harmonious displays in the store windows. Every single detail was scrutinized and carefully curated. In the end, only the ideas were new.

No building is an island. And so, the old department store reflects the Tribsees of today. To symbolize this, we created an indoor rock garden from the rubble of the demolished houses, which was both a wayfinding device and a design element. This was temporarily planted with flowers from the Weber nursery. While our helpers smirked in the beginning, on the opening weekend visitors were amazed when we told them about what they were so excitedly looking at.

When interim uses like these are supported, then people begin to transform a place that has served no purpose in the urban fabric for years. They invest time and sweat capital, make a concrete commitment to the place, and become attached to it. Interim uses can release creative potential in unconventional ways because they are always associated with the temporary. Due to this uncertainty, they are free from the pressure to succeed and can open up spaces for experimentation, with an uncertain outcome and a degree of naivety. This can lead to failure, but also to success. What is certain, however, is that this brings with it valuable practical experience.

T2T—The Way to the Future Is Through the Stomach

In the same manner as the gap between rich and poor, a widening delta between urban and rural areas also seems to be developing. Even the knowledge of how to grow food is fading from many urban minds. This is despite the fact that it satisfies the existential and basic need that we all have—for food. Yet land use and the state of our environment are also directly related to what we eat. According to Wendell Berry,

"eating is an agricultural act." And of course, it is also a political act.

How can we create a new closeness between the land, the food, its producers, and the places where it is consumed, as well as among consumers and one another? In a restaurant that actually isn't one! That is a way to open a rural space to bring people of different backgrounds closer together.

Even though Tribsees hasn't had a restaurant in years, at T2T we didn't just sell straightforward menus, but rather culinary experiences. However, apart from our love for the culinary arts and our pride in the store design, we quickly realized that the real star was the town. Together with local producers, experts, food enthusiasts, and top partners from Hamburg and Berlin, we developed a diverse program for four fantastic days at the end of July.

We played with different formats to build a bridge between our headquarters in Karl-Marx-Straße, the old town center, and the surrounding area. Whether it's a manor house, a fermentation plant, a baroque village, or the dream-come-true of farm ownership: in and around Tribsees there are numerous worthwhile destinations and fascinating people whose appeal extends far beyond the region.

Natural Flavor Enhancers

In big cities, his name is synonymous with the culinary avant-garde, but for most people in Tribsees, Olaf Schnell's vegetable art is still completely unknown. In his case, the place of cultivation and the market are hundreds of kilometers apart. Operating under the name Schnelles Grünzeug (Quick Greens), Olaf from the picturesque village of Dorow grows vegetables for the star kitchens of this country. Through his ingredients and knowledge, completely new worlds of taste have been opened up for us.

Yannic and Susann von Krautkopf convincingly demonstrated to us that these days, it seems that real places can be effortlessly transported via virtual space. With their thousands and thousands of fans on social media, they share their experiences and adventures of life in rural Prebberede, not far from Tribsees. They joined us on the last evening and shared their recipe for thinly sliced beetroot and tender fennel greens on rye bread.

We found other partners almost by chance during our everyday conversations. Municipal employee Nicole Wenzel turned out to be a food blogger on her way to becoming a modern subsistence farmer. She is driven by her dream of her own farm, one that goes beyond growing food to also have an educational purpose. We were lucky to find her, not only for her own agricultural inspiration but because she also led the way to the best cheese in town.

The multitude and variety of our culinary compatriots may come as a surprise when you consider the number of people living in the area. But in this way we not only begin to see the history of urban-rural relations, but also an already existing future of living and working for the people who reside here. Far away from the metropolises, there is far more to be done than just to persevere and preserve. The countryside is not just a landscape, but a state of mind.

The Whole Town Becomes a Restaurant

It quickly became clear that we would not be able to entertain the large number of guests in one evening at one location. And so, we created various formats for different audiences. This situation also helped us to better represent the multidimensional nature of the project.

Thursday was dedicated to all the helpers and sponsors. We opened the doors of the department store to them first, expressing our thanks for their support with small tributes from the kitchen. On Friday, the action shifted to the street, which was closed to traffic every evening. Using various stations, we imitated a food court and rounded off the culinary experience with live music from local musicians. This way, residents and visitors could experience the small town in a different light.

On Saturday, we entirely departed from the established concept of the stationary restaurant and went on a real circuit through the town. During the day, chosen partners in the surrounding countryside opened their doors for our guests and invited everyone to a culinary outing in the country. In the evening, the whole of Tribsees was transformed into an open-air restaurant. We started guided tours in each case with a morsel of culinary art and an introductory talk in the department store. Then groups of about thirty people each moved through the "cinema," "church," and "canoe rest area" stops, and then returned to the "department store."

03

04

05

06

03, 04, 07 Bricks from the dilapidated houses are made into tiles and dishes for the zero-waste restaurant in the former department store. 05, 06 "Only tiling is more beautiful!"—In various workshops, the interior for Tribsees to Table is created in collaboration with students from Recknitz-Trebeltal elementary school, the Trebel Pottery, and local residents. 08, 09 Hilde Zinke from the Trebel Pottery inspects the tile-making worktables.

07

08

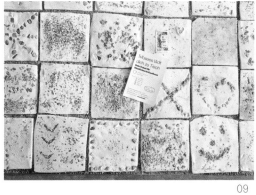

09

10

11

12

10–12 The vacant and partially dilapidated building shines with new luster and charm. 13–15 The whole of Trib-sees is transformed into an open-air restaurant: restaurant patrons walk through the streets of the town on the Trebel, from the cinema to the church (14), to the canoeing rest area (13), and back to the department store.

13

14

15

Both at the actual locations and on the move, the format practically ran itself and proved to be a communication coup. People showed each other that it does not necessarily require the architecture of a built physical space to come together. Here it was the arranged event with its coherent dramaturgy that brought about a long-lost sense of community. Tribsees to Table thus changed the town in a lasting way, not only materially, but also as a collective experience in the memory of residents and visitors. A story that persists and becomes history.

The Essence of Land-Making

"This is the best installation I have seen and experienced since Beuys! And I can say that. Because my friend, Petra Korte, is a salt artist and studied with him back then."
Michael Wunner, Pilgerhus Tribsees

Serious art historians might wrinkle their noses in disgust at such a comparison. But this is also the story of a passionate project beyond the hip and aloof vibe of the big city. Instead, it is at the center of small-town life. The reaction of the observer cited above left us feeling totally embarrassed. Yet it also showed us once again that local residents express their opinions clearly and unambiguously; they do not hold back with their criticisms nor do they dish out praise with anything less than a big shovel.

After months of field research and hands-on work, we can say that "urban practice" can certainly be transferred to rural areas. As in any zone of cultural exchange, conflicts and frictions arise, but so do productive communication and mutual learning. Thus, we may have created something new in Tribsees through our thinking and practices learned in the big city. But we were certainly amazed and enriched by the reactions, questions, and practices of the people of Tribsees.

For us, the direct routes to municipal decision-makers such as the mayor, as well as immediate access to the administration, were very practical advantages. On a personal level, we found it surprising that the sheer abundance of free space in the countryside is in inverse proportion to its absence in the city. Whereas in Hamburg the desire for a little space for self-fulfillment is increasingly pronounced, the people of Tribsees often have so much of it that the seemingly endless green backyards behind their own homes demand their full attention. The needs of residents are different and the sites and modes of addressing them should be chosen accordingly.

Perhaps we could classify Tribsees to Table as a precedent for a rural practice. We served people a future vision for a place believed to be lost—as a socially disguised and inspired artistic culinary practice. During this creative process, we allowed our future audience to become accomplices, thus creating a new public sphere. But we also set up a new approach to "land-making" as a whole. Through active participation and involvement in the project, participants were given the confidence that they had the power to act. And those who have experienced this also realized that they themselves could shape the future.

This is why we are calling for more precedents! For unplanned, spontaneous urban articulations. For leaving open spaces open as well. Interim uses should become an integral part of urban and rural design. What will come out of this in the future? We don't know.

We also didn't know at the beginning of T2T. Would people call us crazy? Would the police evict us? And what would that untraceable Swiss character do to us if they found out about it? Less than a year later, on the night of April 24, 2022, we received this message:

"AS THE OWNER OF KARL-MARX-STRAßE 6, I AM DELIGHTED, AND PERHAPS SOMEONE WILL CONTACT ME DIRECTLY. KIND REGARDS IN THE SPIRIT OF 'PROPERTY IS THEFT! ART IS LIFE!'
ALL THE BEST,
GIOVANNI,
PHONE + 41 ██████ / ████████████ "

To be continued?!

Photos:
Jan Lewandowski: figs. 01, 08, 11–15
Nina Manara: fig. 07
Martha Starke: p. 26; figs. 02–06, 09–10

Tribsees to Table in animated images.

Tribsees/Linz

Illuminated Advertising space&designStrategies Students

Trapped in Linz by the coronavirus, the students translated their visions for Linz into illuminated advertising at the university workshop. Subsequently, about twenty-five light objects were distributed throughout the city.

Karl-Marx-Straße

Stories from Tribsees Siegfried Casper

We were visited over and over again by Mr. Casper, who surprised us with his stories about Tribsees. The number of stories about forgotten pubs, bakeries, hotels, and dance halls was endless. In his private archive there are pictures of almost all buildings from former times—a fascinating collection, which he also likes to show to interested people.

Hotel Tribsees Co-Working Sofie Wagner & Anne Sell

In this quasi-squatted building, Sofie and Anne designed a co-working space as a central location from where they coordinated, planned, and drove everything forward.

Karl-Marx-Straße 27

Tribsees Cinema MattonOffice: Ton, Sofie, Paulus, Anne, Martha & Beate

A public open-air cinema on a vacant lot shows what is possible. An empty wall, two buckets of white paint, electricity from a lantern—and a cinema has already been created in Tribsees. Please bring your own chairs, drinks, and popcorn!

Karl-Marx-Straße 29

Post MattonOffice: Ton, Anne & Sofie

The desires of the residents were col-
lected in a postcard box. Wishes were
addressed to the mayor, the neighbors,
Goethe, the minister, Mr. Scholz, Elon
Musk, their ex-partner, Kant, Dietmar
Bartsch, the baker, Jogi Löw ....
Hundreds of postcards arrived—the
absolute winner was the wish for a
McDonald's.

Tribsees Lounge Martina Del Ben

By placing a counter in the window, Martina created a transition from public space to vacant building. Suddenly, the building was given a "show window" again. The view into the interior invites you to think about all that could take place here!

Improvisation

Just as in Wittenburg (2012) and Gottsbüren (2016), our work here was based on improvisation. It all began with a street in which unsettling elements were used to break through the formality. The space should be, as Christopher Dell describes it in *Improvisations on Urbanity*, permeated with possibilities, possibilities that invite you to anticipate, or even force you to do so.[1] On a normal street, each person behaves ordinarily, as usual. It is only when something happens—say, a truck loaded with chickens breaks down and all the chickens are suddenly scurrying among the pedestrians and cars on the road—that this person has to behave differently, pay closer attention, and perhaps even help recapture the chickens. This could be called "Improvisation Mode 1"—reacting to a deficiency in order to remedy it. Our concern is to plan such deficiencies. To achieve this, it is necessary to enter "Improvisation Mode 2" and intentionally induce people to rethink learned rules and practices. Within the urban planning activity is a search for experimentation. The unexpected is brought out and space is given over to it. To put the small town of Tribsees into Improvisation Mode 2,

we played upon the center, the town became the stage. We did not release scratching chickens into the street in the end. Instead, the residents were to participate as performers in their own stage play and thus contribute to urban development possibilities. Social life was to become visible through words, images, and experiences, as a means of reinforcing this. Through our perspective as outsiders, we were able to encourage people to discuss the problems at hand.

Performative Urbanism
The deeper we delved, the more we discovered things we didn't know. Dealing with that and not feeling distressed by it was one of our strengths. We call this performative urbanism—we invent and act out a world as we would like to see it, and act with a sense of uncertainty as to whether what we are doing will actually lead to that world— with the act itself influencing what we want to explore. Together with artists, students, residents, and various stakeholders, we conducted workshops on the theme "Making Tribsees's Future." Just as in a Potemkin circus, we played with the empty houses, the brownfields, and the public spaces by staging a series of events. New stories and experiences were specifically intended to help us identify and overcome problems using different thoughts and

1   See Christopher Dell, Ton Matton, *Improvisations on Urbanity: Trendy Pragmatism in a Climate of Change,* Rotterdam: Post Editions, 2010, p. 3.

approaches. For example, in this book you will see how a Potemkin pub, a Potemkin cinema ("please bring your own drinks and popcorn"), a Potemkin restaurant, a DIY Potemkin hotel ("furniture available, set up your own room"), a Potemkin museum, a Potemkin gallery, and a Potemkin co-working space all emerged and subsequently permeated the town with new stories. They were all constructed and operated by artists, students, and/or local residents.

Villagers Are Urbanites with Space

Rural issues are very often viewed and judged from an urban perspective. And while the inhabitants of villages and cities are becoming more and more alike due to globalization—we eat the same supermarket food, wear the same chain-store clothes, drive the same brands of cars, watch the same TV programs—there are indeed some differences. And that has nothing to do with stereotyping or prejudices, but rather with the amount of available space and the number of people.

As the Gaussian curve shows, there is always a normal average within a given quantity, with decreasing numbers of outliers to the left and right. The larger the crowd, the larger the normal mass and the greater the quantity of outliers. Thus, in a big city, where there are more people, the extremes are also greater. The poor are poorer, the rich are richer, the left are more left-wing, the right are more right-wing.

In less densely populated rural areas, the demand for specific services is not as great. There are too few people for public transportation, too few children for an elementary school, too few customers for a bakery, a butcher store, or a shoe store, not to mention a croissant shop or a sports shoe store specializing in barefoot shoes. But in some places, there are enough parking spaces in a field for lots of cars along with neighbors who share fresh eggs, raw milk, honey, or cakes. It is very difficult to live an anonymous life in the countryside, it needs a certain amount of respect that goes beyond the usual big city respect for anonymous checkout procedures or pedestrian encounters. When I tell people that I exhibited at the Venice Biennale, within my architect bubble in the city I get instant recognition. But when I tell people about it in the village where I am living, it makes less of an impression; it's related to the very specific field in which I operate. Of course, none of this means that villagers are generally not interested in art or exhibitions; it just means that I am much less likely to meet people with the same interests among this smaller group of people.

Thus, political decisions are necessary in order to ensure that public transportation is available in rural areas, that a stable internet connection is guaranteed, that roads are sufficiently developed, or that there is a sewage system. If such matters were left to the market, they would not be implemented due to a lack of customers. But because we sometimes forget the difference between the needs of city people and villagers, unnecessary things also appear. Asphalt roads are not always needed, a sandy track is sometimes enough in the countryside. If the hole is too big (more on that in a moment), you just drive around it (there is no shortage of space, after all). A sewage system is not always necessary, sometimes a septic tank is sufficient. There is not enough space for that in the city. So, it would make sense to identify these urban-rural differences more clearly. Lack of parking spaces, e-scooter lanes, particulate matter, and noise are also big city problems. In the village, a rooster is allowed to crow, even at four o'clock in the morning.

Condescending Views

What a project like this one in Tribsees reveals is that the condescending view of life in the countryside sometimes held by city dwellers is a source of insecurity. I often hear people say that they are embarrassed to tell people that they are from the countryside. If I move to a village or small town with a group of students, I bring with me just that demographic of eighteen to twenty-five-year-olds that tends to be missing in the countryside. If the students then behave just as they do in the city—for example, by opening a restaurant, squatting houses, roaming around with curiosity, and surprising the neighbors with thousands of questions— then you gradually realize how the self-confidence of the inhabitants increases. I suspect that this could be an important development. If, as statistics show, more and more young people are moving back to the country to raise a family because of the overpriced housing market and the hectic pace of the big city, then they also bring along with them a certain big city mentality. It is precisely this mixture of big city experience and village mindset that could strengthen self-confidence and perhaps lead to smarter developments, which would address the differences between city and countryside.

The Hole in the Road

Speaking of the hole in the road: here I would like to interject an anecdote from my favorite book by Ryszard Kapuściński, *The Shadow of the Sun*. Kapuściński reports on a hole in a road in the Nigerian town Onitsha that resulted in a revival of the place: "In the normally sleepy, lifeless backwater on the outskirts of town, ... there arose, suddenly and spontaneously, thanks solely to that unfortunate hole, a dynamic, humming, bustling neighborhood.

The hole created work for the unemployed, who formed teams of rescuers and made money hauling cars out of the pit. It brought new customers for the women operating the portable sidewalk eateries. ... Social life, too, was reinvigorated: the area around the hole became a place for meetings, conversations, and discussions ...."[2] Kapuściński tells the classic story of the origins of a city, as taught in universities, which comes in many varieties. A ford can be the reason for the emergence of a city, as in the case of Utrecht, Maastricht, or Frankfurt. A dam in a river led to the foundation of Rotterdam and Amsterdam. A castle or a burgh, clearly, is a place that can be well defended, like Hamburg. The name Tribsees probably derives from the Slavic word *treb* or *trebez* (Polish: *trzebiez*), meaning "Gereut," or "clearing." The town is located on an elevated site in a marsh that appears to have been cleared. However, the story for which Tribsees has been known in the media for years is the story of the autobahn with a hole. The A20 has subsided—down into the boggy soil. It reminds me of Kapuściński's story, in which a whole town was built around a hole in the road. From this point of view, the Tribsees hole is a huge opportunity for the town—the site is still only half finished. That means Tribsees still has a few years left to learn from this story about the Nigerian city of Onitsha.

Socialist Utopians

During the Industrial Revolution, the first utopian social ideas also emerged. The goal was to improve living conditions for everyone, and, in particular, for the men, women, and children who worked in factories. Diseases such as cholera raged in the tenements; so living conditions were to be made better by providing light, fresh air, and a little more space.[3] Improved, healthier, and safer working conditions were also created in the workplace. This was better not only for the workers, but also for production and profits.

For some years now, more than half of the world's population has been living in cities, and the trend is rising. Globalization and continued migration to cities have increased the supply of workers, making health a relatively marginal issue. Work has shifted from Western Europe to low-wage countries, where working and living

2   Ryszard Kapuściński: "The Hole in Onitsha," in Ryszard Kapuściński, *The Shadow of the Sun: My African Life,* New York: Vintage Books, 2002, pp. 302–305 [Polish original edition: *Heban,* Warschau: Czytelnik, 1999].

3   To gain a good impression of the living conditions at that time read, for example, George Orwell, *The Road to Wigan Pier,* London: Penguin Books, 2001 [English original edition: London: Victor Gollancz Ltd., 1937].

conditions are still very precarious. For example, at the World Cup construction sites in Qatar, modern-day slaves worked for wages that may have looked good on paper, but, in reality, were seriously diminished by housing and food costs. For every factory worker who keels over from exhaustion, there is always a replacement ready. In Europe, for example, there are many professions for which trade unions have hardly any significance, such as courier and express services workers. It seems that the supply of workers and the privatization process are too great. How can we, reader and author, look each other in the eye when we know that the clothes we are wearing were most likely made by modern-day slaves in a polluting factory? Even if organic and fair-trade labels are emblazoned on the products, this is no guarantee (maybe for the brand, but not for the clothes themselves).[4]

The Brazilianization of the World
The "Brazilianization of the world," as Ulrich Beck described it, has been taking place for a long time.[5] We take all utilities for granted: drinking water,

electricity, heating, waste disposal—everything is so well organized that these assets are no longer noticed. The current natural gas crisis shows that these things are not assured, and that we may have to accept reductions in these areas of supply as well. A heated home and a heated workplace can no longer be thought of as givens, just as pensions, social security, and the health care system are no longer accessible to everyone as standard practice. Some neoliberal governments are even saying that you have to provide for your own pension, without any apologies for jettisoning this major achievement of nineteen-fifties politics, which was fought hard for at the time. Already, many small business owners cannot afford the cost of health insurance. The current rate of inflation is also reminiscent of the nineteen-eighties in Brazil, when people rushed to the supermarket as soon as their salaries were paid at the end of the month, because the currency would lose much of its value by the next day. I still remember how, during my internship in Rio, I stood in line for hours at the checkout in a supermarket with about a hundred checkouts—everyone had two to three shopping carts full.

Comfort
For decades, the pursuit of ever more comfort has been par for the course but the downside of this comfortable life is becoming more and more

4   See Dana Thomas, *Deluxe: How Luxury Lost Its Luster,* London: Penguin Books, 2007.
5   "Brazilianization of the West," see: Ulrich Beck, *The Brave New World of Work,* Cambridge: Polity Press, 2000 [German original edition: *Schöne neue Arbeitswelt,* Frankfurt am Main: Campus Verlag, 1999].

apparent. The economy is based on squandering resources and energy; it is only sustained by a financial bubble that floats on the labor of countless workers who toil for a pittance, caught in the economic trap of trade barriers, work permits, rules, and laws. This has been commonplace for some time, but via the internet and globalization, we face it every day— climate change, child labor, modern slavery, and food contamination, just to name a few extremes. This daily confrontation generates a feeling of unease across broad segments of society.

A slow urban planning aims to resist this comfort model devised by a small elite group at the expense of a growing underclass. Slow urban planning wants to join the tradition of utopian thinkers such as Charles Fourier, Robert Owen, or even Upton Sinclair.[6]

6   See: Upton Sinclair, *The Jungle*, New York: Doubleday, 1906.

Karl-Marx-Straße

Synchronized Ironing Party Tribsees Women's Association

A grand opening with wrinkled table-cloths was absolutely unthinkable. As a result, many people responded to the impromptu call from the Women's Association and ironed a hundred meters of tablecloth. The fuse blew five times because seven irons were being used at the same time. That was a bit too much for our improvised power supply in this quasi-squatted building.

Südmauerstraße

Karl-Marx-Straße 21

German Property Shop Anna Weberberger

Obj. Nr. 002

Modernes Holzhaus, energieeffizient
In der Tribseeser Innenstadt, unweit vom zentralen Marktplatz entfernt, wird dieses totalsanierte Objekt zur Selbstnutzung oder Kapitalanlage angeboten! Besonders ansprechend die moderne minimalistische Holzfassade, bis in die Räume hinein sichtbar. Die Außenwände besitzen einen 16 cm starken Vollwärmeschutz der Wärmeleitgruppe 035. Diese sowie die am Flach-dach neu angebrachte PV-Anlage ermöglichen die beneidenswert hohe Energieeffizienz (Klasse A++) des Objekts.

PKW-Stellplatz inkl.!

Einmaliger Kaufpreis auf Anfrage
zzgl. Courtage: 3,75 % inkl. MwSt

Obj. Nr. 059

Bürogebäude zu verkaufen
Zum Angebot stehen lichtdurchflutete Büroflächen in der Innenstadt, sehr verkehrsgünstig gelegen und daher besonders gut geeignet für Anwaltskanzleien und Consultingunternehmen. Das Haus ist ein teilsaniertes Gebäude mit Bossenputz-Fassade und Fahrstuhl. Dank des offenen Grundrisses lässt sich das Objekt in individuelle Büroräumlichkeiten aufteilen und vermieten.

Sanitäranschluss möglich!

Einmaliger Kaufpreis auf Anfrage
zzgl. Courtage: 3,75 % inkl. MwSt

Karl-Marx-Straße 25

Tribsees Gallery Paulus Goerden

Chinese Takeout

02/24/2038 Post by the successful influencer L.

... in which Mr. Y. (MY) tells the story of his immigration and integration.

We see Mr. Y. at the stove preparing a mutton stew in his kitchen. He has opened an informal restaurant in his own house.

L: Do you cook?

MY: Yes, with a passion, using organic ingredients. Let me tell you that when I came to Tribsees, even something as simple as salt was actually incredibly dirty, a polluted food. It was full of metal residues and other toxic substances. Every single foodstuff was still subject to regulatory standards, but if you added it all up, all the ingredients you used in every dish, then every meal was a kind of toxic bomb. So, I opened a restaurant here in Tribsees to prepare honest dishes.

L: A restaurant?

MY: Yes, just like that, spontaneously, in the living room. Almost all my neighbors have started small businesses. This mutton, for example, comes from a neighbor, direct from the pasture behind us. I also get eggs and chicken here, as well as fish, tomatoes, and milk.

I actually landed here in Tribsees by chance. I had sold goldfish to a resident of Bad Sülze via the internet. At that time, I was still living in Guangzhou. But there were some problems at the European border—too much bromine in the pallets on which the aquariums were stacked. So, the fish were not permitted to enter the country. Then

Katrin, my customer, just came by and picked them up herself—and that's how we got to know each other. When I later came to Tribsees, everything was very run-down. I remember the IKEA advertisement at the time, it was part of my integration course: "Are you still dwelling, or are you really living?" The teacher told us how Germans lived, and we made jokes about boring suburban developments. But then this slogan was unleashed on spatial planning. I don't remember exactly how, but in any case, the minister introduced us to slow urban planning in Mecklenburg-Vorpommern. The land-use plan was scrapped after a referendum. Restrictions were no longer imposed, and instead, possibilities were expanded. People were allowed to produce things in and around their houses. A multitude of pancake houses, restaurants, wine-tasting rooms, riding stables, children's farms, and the like

sprang up. All were highly individual, and to a large extent also a response to the inflation and energy crisis of 2022. Many tried to earn some extra income through their hobbies. Not all succeeded, of course, but this triggered some exciting changes in how we produced and consumed. The vertical farming high-rise was built at that time, for example. Much more could then be produced using much less energy. This was done locally, requiring minimal transport, and minimal water and nutrients for the plants—very efficient and yet still organic. Over there on the corner, a man sells rubber boats, boots, and life jackets, etc., mainly as souvenirs for international tourists who come here to gaze at the bogs. I can buy bread on the street, as well as rice, fish, black beans, and plantains. And of course, wine—real wine from Pomerania.

Neubaustraße

Mirror Bricks Maya Leen

At the corner of the old warehouse, this reflection-inducing work was created from mirror bricks. What is the situation in the city and how do you deal with it? These are the questions that Maya Leen poses with her work.

garnelen / shrimps

Karl-Marx-Straße 5

Echoes Bipin Rao & Jonathan Holstein

The two Wismar lighting designers Bipin Rao and Jonathan Holstein brought light to some of the dark derelict buildings as well as the work Echoes, as seen here next to the former department store. Not only their lighting, but also their idiosyncratic energy as musicians and DJs provided some points of light during the project.

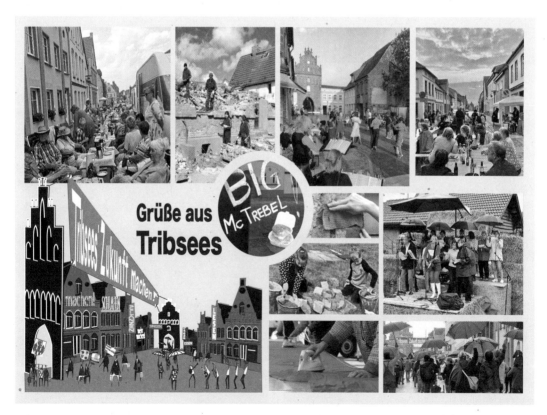

zwischen den beiden Toren von Tribsees suchen

70 leere Häuser nach neuen Tribseesern !

Sülzer Chaussee 18

Mural Alexandra Babišová

At the mayor's request,
Alexandra Babišová
painted this mural on the
old building belonging to
the municipal yard. Had
he known how fast and
beautifully she could do
it, she would have been
allowed to cover the
whole building with this
mural.

Neubaustraße

I love TRI Nasrin Qmoniri

Roughly based on the
slogan "I amsterdam"
Nasrin built this selfie-
ode to Tribsees. As in
Amsterdam, the letters
were removed again in
Tribsees, but not, in my
opinion, because too
many tourists were taking
selfies.

Papenstraße

Karl-Marx-Straße

Graffiti Tribsees Youth Club

The youth wanted a graffiti workshop. The walls we put up on a vacant lot attracted many young people who were able to express their creativity using a can of spray paint.

Papenstraße 13

Balcony MattonOffice & Florian Gwinner

This podium was created from the remains of a collapsed building. The minister and the mayor had no objections to opening the Tribsees Centennial from this improvised lectern, even though this spot does not exactly put the best face on Tribsees. Or does it? It shows exactly the kind of potential it has and clearly demonstrates the energy with which Tribsees is tackling its future.

Linz Works Vahdeta Tahirovic, Nikita Narder & Celeste Montales

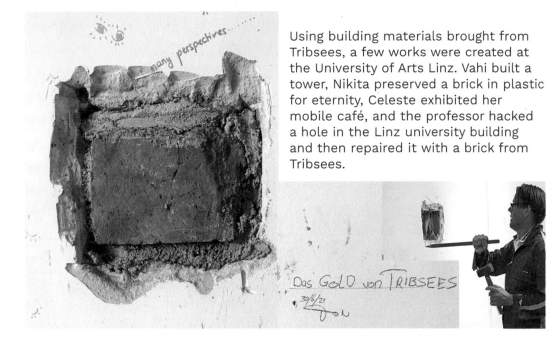

Using building materials brought from Tribsees, a few works were created at the University of Arts Linz. Vahi built a tower, Nikita preserved a brick in plastic for eternity, Celeste exhibited her mobile café, and the professor hacked a hole in the Linz university building and then repaired it with a brick from Tribsees.

Das GOLD von TRIBSEES
30/6/21

Wind Turbines

... in which the grandson of Mr. C. (MCG) talks about his grandfather's private archive.

We see Mr. C.'s grandson strolling down the street and pointing to each of the wind turbines.

MCG: Yes, my grandfather told me that there used to be antennas everywhere here, some of which were even secretly set up so that people could watch West German television. Then came the satellite dishes, my mother told me, which in turn disappeared with the expansion of the fiber optic network. And now we have all these "turbies," small wind turbines on the roof, wind spheres, wind rotors, wind turbines, and I don't even know what all of them are called. These are connected to the Worldwide Energy Web, which means that when there is too little wind, the electricity is sourced from elsewhere. And if too much is produced, it is sent somewhere else.

L: Do people also earn money from these?

MCG: Yes, you can make money by producing more than you consume. But more importantly, the morally driven approaches to energy saving of the fossil fuel era are over. So much is produced that we no longer need to conserve electricity—it's abundant. This is also because we have learned that we can get by with less. Not watching TV one evening is no problem at all,

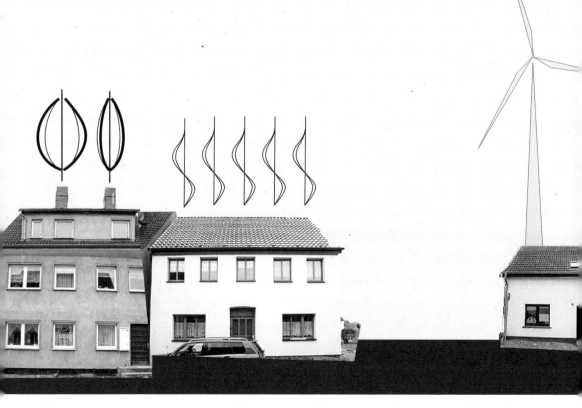

the refrigerator can be turned off in the winter—an outdoor cupboard is perfectly adequate then. And since the gas crisis of 2022, it's also become totally normal to turn down the heating and to turn on the stove less often, and wearing bulky sweaters is very much in vogue. Of course, some are still opposed to these small wind turbines, but fortunately not as many as in the past, back when even death threats were made against politicians. Since society is no longer so extremely neoliberal because decisions are no longer made over people's heads, and because participation and safety are at the forefront of planning processes, there is less resistance. We don't all have to agree in order to live together, do we? For example, the woman next door is very nice, but she keeps pigs, which as a vegan I don't agree with at all. But she takes good care of them, the animals in fact enjoy a happy life with her—it's just a bit too short ... And there, a little further down the street, lives someone who has completely disconnected his house from the power grid. He watches TV, listens to the radio, and indeed does everything on his cell phone, which uses almost no electricity; a small hand-crank generator is sufficient. He doesn't have a refrigerator, and with the drone supermarket delivery service, he doesn't really need one anymore. Almost like back in the nineteen-fifties, when, as my grandfather told me, the baker, the butcher, and the milkman delivered to your door every day. Back then, my grandmother wrote down her shopping list for the next day in a little notebook, now the vegetable drone comes every day and delivers orders placed through the shopping app. Once again, milk is also being delivered here fresh every day. It comes from that building over there. Look, over there you see happy cows grazing on the third floor.

Self-Sufficient Living

08/15/2051 Post by successful influencer L.

... in which a municipal official (MO) talks about a new way of living in Tribsees.

We can see a zoning map on her computer screen.

MO: We learned from the financial and inflation crises and developed a new land-use plan. Instead of overly expensive houses for people with steady jobs, the plan specified very simple cottages for people who can't or don't want to live according to the neoliberal model of comfort. These houses sit on generous plots of land—like allotments where you can grow your own food—with a cellar to store your produce. A rainwater harvesting system provides water for showers. The system regulates the amount of water so that dry spells can be easily managed. A composting toilet replaces the sewer system and provides compost for the garden. Electricity comes from local wind turbines and from the cogeneration unit in the basement. A small multifuel stove with secondary burn keeps the living room cozy.

Of course, there are no public parking lots in the neighborhood and no public lighting or playgrounds with any of that standardized playground equipment for children. The whole so-called convenience model with its thousands of superfluous rules has been replaced by a personal sense of responsibility on the part of each individual. There is a right of way for adjoining properties, and in addition to that, a set of rules that people agree upon themselves. In case of disagreement, the matter is submitted to the Reasonableness Jury. These are houses without infrastructure connections. Land sales were at fair prices and speculation was out of the question because of the unusual site location. The houses were built on moorland because they were to have an agricultural function; small-scale farming in the yard was to supply local

produce to the organic stores in the area. There was an unexpectedly large demand for these simple houses.

Scene change: here we see Ms. D. H. (MDH) describing the decisive change of direction in her life.

MDH: No, I can't complain. I've gotten my life back on track. It was different a few years ago. As many chickens as I've slaughtered in my life, you wouldn't think it would be possible. I had to do it, I needed the job at the slaughterhouse to pay off my mortgage, to pay for daycare. Every month almost 2,000 euros just vanished ... and then the costs for insurance, food, and drink didn't exactly go down!
In the end, energy costs were so high that this was no longer manageable. The good transportation connections were one of the reasons why I bought my house at the time. But that was before the oil crisis of 2022. The high-quality public transport that we had been promised when we bought a house in the development was a lie—there was only an occasional municipal bus.
L: And that was sold as high-quality living?

MDH: Exactly, so I made radical changes in my life. I quit my job and sold the so-called sustainable suburban house. Fortunately, that was just before the wave of inflation really took off. In Tribsees I came across this very small cottage. Without any unnecessaryluxuries, it was very simple, but also very environmentally conscious. There is an additional stove in the living room, in which I burn a piece of peat in the evening. This heating is connected to the cogeneration plant, which also provides electricity. It is really, very environmentally friendly and clean. Every spring I trade some peat for eggs with my neighbor down the street. I use eggs from traditional free-range farms. Just like in the old days when everything was still called "sustainable" and "organic." My contented chickens run free on the farm and lead the most species-appropriate life for a domestically bred chicken. Every year, when bird flu makes it necessary to keep them indoors again, I bring them into the green chicken coop, where they are safe. And yes, occasionally I bring a rooster to my neighbor. He has a Chinese restaurant over there and still does his own butchering, so at least you know what you're eating.

Papenstraße

Papenstraße 13

Colors from Tribsees Silvia Corral Fernández

Silvia designed this wall in a very colorful way, without being afraid of large, open spaces.

Papenstraße 13

Participatory City Weiqi Wang

For two weeks, together with children from Tribsees, artist Weiqi Wang built a city out of old bricks. They thought about their wishes and made designs for them using available construction debris. A city full of ideas for the future was created. After the workshop, the children continued in their blue overalls, got bricks and clay from the dilapidated houses next door, and built:

a swimming pool, an animal farm, a
cinema, a theater, a balloon airport,
a train station, and all the things a
small town needs nowadays. They took
their cue from the punk band Palais

Schaumburg: "Wir bauen eine neue
Stadt. Gibst du mir Wasser, rühr ich den
Kalk!" (We're building a new town. If you
give me water, I'll stir the lime!).

How People Have to Live

The vacancy rate in many small towns and villages threatens social life. Stores are closing, clubs are disbanding, too few children are going to school. This is a phenomenon that is not unique to Mecklenburg-Vorpommern; it can be observed all over the world. In Tribsees, it manifests itself in a virulent form. Even before reunification there were abandoned houses here. They stood unheeded and now, over thirty years later, they are dilapidated and in ruins. Leaking gutters or collapsed roofs have allowed nature to slowly reclaim the spaces once occupied by people. Within some houses a small birch grove has grown up as pioneer vegetation. Only piles of rubble remain as evidence of some houses, and sometimes even these have been disposed of and obliterated with parking lots or anonymous lawns.

Shrinking Cities

The atmosphere in this kind of living environment deteriorates and enters a vicious circle. In the international study *Shrinking Cities*, Jörg Dürrschmidt writes: "Euphoria about innovative urban planning ideas such as the 'perforated patchwork city' are out of place as long as it is not understood that wastelands in terms of people's life worlds are also part of the problem, and that these cannot be simply 'rearranged,' 'reduced,' or 'recolonized.' For the discourse of everyday life, the apparently calculable 'positive shrinkage' is portrayed more as an incalculable loss of identity and meaning. Each demolition is not only an adjustment made to the level of vacancy, it is also always a gap in the 'collective memory,' which mainly consists of spatial images of those who are (still) there."[1] In Tribsees, too, many of the remaining residents romanticize about a time when the town was still lively and the streets were still full, when life happened in public and neighbors met each other on the street. "There used to be seven dance halls on Karl-Marx-Straße," our neighbor Mr. Casper told us several times. He knew them all and showed us pictures from his private town archive, in which each house is described. A longing for social togetherness is palpable.

Ulf Matthiesen outlines some relevant development trends: "Crisis-ridden small and midsize regional centers increasingly lack the human resources needed to develop a critical mass that would stabilize the decline in population and create competency for the region. In contrast to earlier waves of out-migration, this situation threatens to create a knowledge-society competency trap in places with weak structures. … Under the pressure caused by crises and

1 Jörg Dürrschmidt, "Shrinkage Mentality," in Philipp Oswalt, ed., *Shrinking Cities*, volume 1, Ostfildern-Ruit: Hatje Cantz, 2004, pp. 274–279, on p. 274.

exacerbated by brain drain, local networks tend to become isolated. This reinforces the 'weakness of strong ties.' The result is the formation of networks that do nothing in the long run to spur the dynamics of innovation, but instead mainly work toward maximizing their own interests."[2] However, the mobility radius has increased once again in recent decades due to the further development of globalization and mobilization, meaning that Tribsees has now almost become a suburb of Rostock. For work, local residents drive all the way to Rostock. Some of the young people who once left as soon as they had their driver's licenses have since started families and are now considering returning to Tribsees—or are actually coming back, but not necessarily to an old apartment in the run-down town center, but rather to one of the surrounding new housing developments.

Embellishment through Creative Milieus

In many large cities, artists and alternative types are moving into houses similar to those in Wittenburg, Gottsbüren, or Tribsees in their search for affordable studios and living spaces. In the publication *Dorf machen!* (Make a Village!) I described pre-gentrification as follows: It is just this class in our society that lives in the sense of possibility, in this utopia that does not shy away from reality but treats it as an invention. In Mecklenburg-Vorpommern, however, the alternative scene as it exists in Hamburg or Berlin is marginal, and as the Gauss curve also shows, does not have the minimum quantity to form a scene. There are a few artists, a few free spirits, and those few small existing stores that are struggling to survive. The population is relatively old. The youth are disappearing from rural areas, going off to find work as soon as they get a driver's license.[3] Policies driven by local interests, as defined by economist Richard Florida in his 2002 bestseller *The Rise of the Creative Class*, by which cities embellish themselves with creative milieus in order to create an invest-ment-friendly image, could attract new investors, both those with money and a sense of reality as well as those with social commitment and a sense of possibility.[4] Gentrification—fought against as a negative development in many big cities and criticized by Christoph Twickel as part of a mechanism that regulates

2 Ulf Matthiesen, "Gone: Human Capital in Eastern Germany," in Philipp Oswalt, ed., *Shrinking Cities*, volume 1, Ostfildern-Ruit: Hatje Cantz, 2004, pp. 172–173, on p. 173.

3 See Ton Matton, "Prä-Gentrifizierung", in Matton, ed., *Dorf machen*, p. 76.
4 See Richard Florida, *The Rise of the Creative Class*, New York: Basic Books, 2002.

participation in the city through money and social background— could be just the right concept for Mecklenburg-Vorpommern in a rural and "cozy" form.[5] The pioneers, students, artists, bohemians, and alternative cultures are, according to Twickel, the lubricant of the political class, the construction industry, real estate funds, banks, and investors. In rural areas, these pioneers and the political class are very close to each other. For this kind of emancipation, the countryside simply lacks the mass of like-minded people. Here, you cannot submerge yourself in the narrow biotope of your own bubble, like you can in a metropolis, because here this biotope simply does not exist.

Respect

In the countryside, you depend on more than just your own scene.[6] The social control often criticized by city dwellers is called respect in the countryside. People depend on each other, even if they don't lead the same lifestyle. Residents today are predominantly older people from the same social class. In this way, they form a threshold, sometimes unknowingly. Gentrification could help to rekindle their sense of identity and their appeal to outsiders. In a kind of trendy, pragmatic way, you could say that villages and small towns need to "pre-gentrify," first by attracting artists and alternative types who rediscover the vacant buildings, who will then, when the situation really picks up, be subsequently displaced by global firms. However, some things have changed in this regard as well. You might say that the differences are no longer as striking as they were a few decades ago. With electricity, television, cars, mobile phones, and faster internet connections, life in the countryside is looking more and more like life in the big city. Traditional working conditions have disappeared, and more and more work takes place in front of the computer screen; both the office worker and the farm woman riding her tractor work on their computers. Bread comes from factories, milk from industrialized farms. The countryside is urbanized. Today, you eat the same supermarket food in the village as in the city, live with the same IKEA furnishings, watch the same Netflix series and TV programs, do your shopping in the same online store, and—just like in the city—you have the feeling, thanks to Facebook, that there's more going on elsewhere. In this respect, too, city

5   See Christoph Twickel, *Gentrifidingsbums oder Eine Stadt für alle*, Hamburg: Edition Nautilus, 2010.
6   Ton Matton, ed., *Dorf machen*, n.p. (Blog des Professors, 20. Juni 2015 – 8.00 Uhr).

and country are no different. People are no longer as dependent on each other locally because they are much more active in social media. You can live next to each other instead of with each other. Many people are in their own parallel world, in the city as well as in the country.

A New Narrative

Richard Florida critiqued his own gentrification theory and rethought it.[7] He recognized that a new narrative needed to be developed that is not just about creative and innovative growth, but rather recognized how inclusion is a part of prosperity. His formula has proven beneficial to those who are already affluent, mostly white, and middle class; it has fueled rampant real estate speculation, displaced the bohemians he so fetishized, and allowed the problems that once plagued downtown areas to simply migrate to the suburbs. After years of propagandizing loft apartments and shabby-chic cafés, Richard Florida's eyes have been opened to the dark side of returning to the city. *The New Urban Crisis* paints a bleak picture of what he calls "winner-take-all urbanism," describing the rise of "superstar cities" like New York, London, and Tokyo.[8] This gentrification effect is already noticeable in Tribsees as well. While we were still implementing our projects and initiatives, the price of some local real estate increased. The owners hoped that the project would stimulate greater demand, which was immediately reflected in the asking price.

In the above-mentioned *Der Spiegel* interview,[9] Klara Geywitz mentions some of the problems that people will have to face in the near future. The human-induced increase in greenhouse gases and associated climate change were already prompting people to question the consumption of meat from large farms. Vehicles that run on fossil fuels should be restricted. Space requirements per person should be reduced again to twenty-five square meters instead of the fifty square meters that the average person now occupies, she noted. The most frequently used rooms, she observed, are the bedroom, bathroom, and

7 Oliver Wainwright: "'Everything Is Gentrification Now': But Richard Florida Isn't Sorry" (2017), *The Guardian*, https://www.theguardian.com/cities/2017/oct/26/gentrification-richard-florida-interview-creative-class-new-urban-crisis (accessed March 6, 2023).

8 See Richard Florida, *The New Urban Crisis: How Our Cities Are Increasing Inequality, Deeping Segregation, and Failing the Middle Class—and What We Can Do About It*, New York: Basic Books, 2017.

9 "Bauministerin Geywitz über Sanierungspflicht von Immobilien," pp. 30–33.

kitchen. Reducing the amount of living space required per capita has many advantages. Modern housing concepts could, for example, combat loneliness in cities. She envisions large urban neighborhoods with smaller apartment floorplans and larger or greater numbers of common areas for everyone. Politics cannot and should not dictate how people should live, she concluded.

I don't quite agree with the latter observation, however. Politicians have been writing laws regulating housing for over a hundred years. For example, there is a regulation as to how big a window should be so that enough light and fresh air can enter the dwelling. There are rules that specify precisely how high and deep a step should be so that you don't fall. If you do not follow these rules, you won't get a building permit. On the one hand, such rules restrict individual freedom—or abstract freedom, as Hegel termed it—that is, the ability to do what you want independent of social rules and norms.[10] This also implies the potential of occasionally violating these rules and norms. In exchange, these serve our social freedom—or, as per Hegel, concrete freedom—the freedom that is maintained by rules and norms so that freedom is possible for all. Thus, if you build a very steep staircase or use a rope ladder, more people may fall and need to be hospitalized than if you had used standardized stairs. Consequently, a rope ladder is not allowed in dwellings. However, it seems that this individual, abstract freedom is getting out of hand not only in Minister Geywitz's thinking, but also across society as a whole, which is becoming vehemently more individualistic.

Forbidden

Land-use planning has become more and more specialized and detailed over the past couple of centuries. It is striking, however, that by far most rules are formulated as prohibitions.[11] The reason that they prohibit so many things is that a middle-of-the-road approach has become the standard. There is a fear of disruption, a fear that something might occur that you don't want: noise, dirt, danger. This leads to more and more prohibitions being established, which have social freedom as their ultimate goal. However, because the fear that something unwanted could happen predominates, they are more likely

10   See "Erster Teil: Das abstrakte Recht" and "Dritter Teil: Die Sittlichkeit," in Georg Wilhelm Friedrich Hegel: *Grundlinien der Philosophie des Rechts,* Hamburg: Felix Meiner Verlag, 2017 [German original edition: Berlin: Nicolaische Buchhandlung, 1820].

11   Ton Matton / Schie 2.0: *Regelland,* as part of the exhibition *unlimited.nl-2* (guest curator: Hou Hanru), De Appel Gallery, Amsterdam January 22–March 21, 1999.

to bring about social restrictions. There is a need for an evolutionary planning system that responds to changing social processes, because in the globalized world the small unit is becoming more and more important. Since the modern era, urban planning has traditionally specified various zones: residential areas, industrial areas, traffic flows, recreational areas—all strictly separated from each other and elaborated through an extensive set of rules so that they do not interfere or disturb each other. The height and placement of the garden wall facing the neighbors are dictated to the centimeter. How much smoke a barbecue grill is allowed to produce is specified, as is the fact that dandelions are not allowed to spread to the neighbor's garden. In the meantime, everything has been planned so thoroughly that it is hardly possible to build a wind turbine because all of the rules clog up the space like an arterial blockage. Many architects and technocrats believe in this modernist approach, which, however, brings new problems with every solution. A technical escape from this misery appears to be readily available, as reports in the (social) media suggest, if each individual just bears a small part of their professional responsibility. But such escapist behavior is no longer possible in a globalized world. Peter Sloterdijk expressed his great confidence in architects at the 2009 World Climate Conference in Copenhagen. They already had the solutions to climate change in their files, he said. LinkedIn and Instagram provide a clear picture of what architects have in their files. Unfortunately, I have to disagree with Sloterdijk. There are indeed many solutions in those files: buildings made of wood and clay with extra insulating glass, intelligent energy recovery concepts, air-purifying facade elements, green roofs and facades, flood protection facades. There are countless solutions to countless problems. However, such solutions are almost always singular, while the problems are interwoven. An ecosystem depends on many factors that are all interconnected. Trying to solve these problems separately through technological feats sounds good on LinkedIn and often looks great on Instagram, but utterly trivializes the causes and consequences of climate change. All such architecture labeled "sustainable" is still a massive contributor to climate change. It's more like the greenwashing of the big multinationals. Suddenly, an oil and gas company is sustainable because it invests heavily in solar and wind energy, but now more oil is flowing than ever before. A fast food chain recycles, but meanwhile is still cutting down the Amazon rainforest so its soon-to-be-hamburger cattle can graze, and a hotel is sustainable these days just because it doesn't wash the towels every day. It's time, as Pedro Gadanho wrote, for architecture to change, to go from being a destroyer to a contributor.[12]

Chaos Theory

According to chaos theory, the flap of a butterfly's wings in Brazil could conceivably cause a tornado in Texas. What would this mean for our architects, how could their wingbeats trigger a tornado? After all, we are talking about so-called star architects here, who dictate what global architecture looks like. What if these stars took their role as societal models seriously? I can imagine Rem Koolhaas constructing his next iconic building out of bamboo, which he himself would have planted in an allotment on the thirty-seventh floor of a "delirious" New York skyscraper back in the early nineteen-seventies. In his office, all employees would follow a vegan diet and walk or bike to work. They would be dressed in fair trade clothing made of ecological materials (not black, because the dye needed for the architect's typical clothing causes too much groundwater pollution in the countries where it is produced).

During fitness classes, these architects could produce enough energy to run the office computers. Every now and then they would cultivate new bamboo groves for their next iconic project. What effect would this have on their successors and copycat offices? The world would look different

Through the flapping of her wings, Greta Thunberg has touched off a Fridays for Future whirlwind. The demand that government leaders finally do what they have been promising for years, namely, to keep climate change under control, goes down well with many politicians because their role, their ability, is not being questioned. The demand is: you promised, now you have to keep your promise. The naivety of this demand is slowly becoming apparent, and the debate is becoming sharper. The innocent Fridays for Future are turning into a somewhat more aggressive form of civil disobedience, as shown for example by the recent Extinction Rebellion protests, where climate activists superglue their hands to artworks and highways to rebel against extinction.

Since all multinational companies certainly mean well and architects are already doing the best they can with their technical solutions, the realization is slowly dawning that our comfort level needs to be lowered. The current gas crisis has already led to suggestions to turn down the

12   Pedro Gadanho, *Climax Change! How Architecture Must Transform in the Age of Ecological Emergency*, New York/Barcelona: Actar Publishers, 2022.

heating a few degrees and put on a thick sweater. Back in the nineteen-nineties, the Talking Heads illustrated how ecological thinking is changing society in "(Nothing but) Flowers": the big parking lot has turned into a peaceful oasis; daisies now grow where Pizza Hut used to be. David Byrne sang about wanting a lawn mower because he couldn't get used to this lifestyle: "Once there were parking lots. Now it's a peaceful oasis … This was a Pizza Hut. Now it's all covered with daisies. … This was a discount store. Now it's turned into a cornfield. … Don't leave me stranded here. I can't get used to this lifestyle."[13] Meanwhile, it's no longer a question of whether we want these changes, but of how we approach the problem of shaping these changes so that we can thrive among them.

Doing Without

But it is just as naive to believe in doing without. Since the founding of the Club of Rome and its report *The Limit to Growth*, which is now over fifty years old, there has always been talk in the context of ecological thinking of doing without, of reduction: reducing waste, reducing energy consumption, reducing carbon dioxide. This is a radical call for moral action. But first, this is not a very pleasant thing to do; secondly, it is never enough;

thirdly, it runs counter to our natural developmental behavior, and finally—as has long since been proven—it does not work. During the past half-century, our energy consumption has doubled, and our waste production has increased even more. The area of desert has roughly doubled, while the area of forest cover has roughly halved. So, what would be a smart way to proceed?

Decades of technological developments demonstrate a wide range of solutions. The unacceptable sanitary conditions of the early twentieth century were improved. Air pollution, which caused acid rain and the eutrophication of rivers, was mitigated by fine dust filters in chimneys and sewage treatment plants in cities. These technological successes have seemingly led to technology no longer being seen as a tool but becoming the goal itself. In *Risk Society*, German sociologist Ulrich Beck writes that money is no longer enough to buy security.[14] Like nuclear energy and terrorism, climate change effects will exceed the limits of what can be solved with money. No gated community, no walled city can tackle these problems alone. Bruno Latour expands the concept of territory

13   Talking Heads, "(Nothing but) Flowers," 1988, Warner Bros. Records Inc., single cover.

14   Ulrich Beck, *Risk Society: Towards a New Modernity*, London: Sage Publications, 1992 [German original edition: *Risikogesellschaft. Auf dem Weg in eine andere Moderne*, Frankfurt am Main: Suhrkamp, 1986].

to include everything we depend
on, including all related aspects
such as clean air, carbon dioxide,
groundwater, clean soil.[15] Thus,
the architect who builds on a plot
supplied by pipes and cables should
also consider (and be responsible
for) the effects that construction has
on the air, the earth, the water, the
climate, the biotope, and so on. This
concerns the building site as much
as the places from which it draws
resources. The famous saying that
stood for unlimited possibility in the
era of the first skyscrapers—"The sky
is the limit"—changes to "The sky is
the limit." The possibilities are in fact
limited!

15   Bruno Latour, *Das Parlament der Dinge:
Für eine politische Ökologie*, Frankfurt am Main:
Suhrkamp, 2009 [French original edition:
Politiques de la nature, Paris: Éditions La
Découverte & Syros, 1999].

IM
BESTAND
DENKEN

KLEINSTADT
UND
LEERSTAND
ERFAHRBAR
MACHEN

TRIBSEES
STEHT MODELL

Wem gehören
die Häuser,
die Plätze und
Straßen von
Tribsees?

Foto: © Anna Weberberger

Papenstraße 13

Barmacy Sebastian Dorfer & Tobias Leibetseder

From old pieces of scrap Sebastian and
Tobias built a bar for the opening of the
Centennial. With shots and vaccination
stamps.

Katharinenberg

The Sun Was Here Tomiris Dmitrievskikh

The light of the setting sun shines through a hole in the roof. With this work, Tomiris Dmitrievskikh appears to be trying to give the people of Tribsees a little hope for their town. Or is this really about the downfall of Tribsees?

Papenstraße 13

Brick City MattonOffice: Paulus, Basti, Lilo & Anna

Together with the Trebeltal Local Development Association, students built a model of Tribsees. These were initially made from cardboard, while many stories and anecdotes were being told. Then Paulus built the model again using Tribsees bricks and fluorescent paint to create an exhibition piece for the Centennial. It gives a good overview of just how much of the town seventy empty houses represent: almost thirty percent of the buildings here are empty and disintegrating!

Karl-Marx-Straße 50

Grand Hotel Tribsees MattonOffice: Chaz, Anna & Timur

We created a DIY hotel from old furniture in some of the empty buildings. All visitors were allowed to furnish their rooms themselves. The bathrooms all consisted of a coffee pot with bowls.

Climate-Friendly Woodland

08/15/2044 Post by the successful influencer L.

..., in which Ms. d. B.'s (MDB) initiative for a bog woodland is explained.

We see a wooden shed. An amphibious tractor is parked in front of it in the bog woodland. We hear L.'s voice off-camera.

L: Ms. d. B. lives in the Tribseeser Moor. She has started an initiative to plant a bog woodland there. Located directly adjacent to Rostock-Laage Airport, travelers living in Germany can plant a tree with her live online, which she will then care for on their behalf. Or travelers can get the cuttings delivered to their homes to plant in their own wetland gardens. Through this initiative, the phenomenon of carbon offsetting is becoming an aspect of regional planning.

The camera gives us a view over the landscape. We see trees in flowerpots in the foreground and woodland in the background. A wide variety of trees can be discerned—from bog oak to bog banana, and everything in between.

L: I wonder what the person who cut down the last tree on Easter Island must have thought? Did they have any idea that this would also destroy the island's culture?
MDB: In 2025, I started my tree-planting campaign. I heard on the news that people were planting trees in Zaire to offset the carbon dioxide from their air travel. However, these were already cut down again two years later by poor farmers desperately searching for arable land. Now I have already planted about 50,000 trees myself. I offer them to

people who travel by plane and want to see their tree of absolution grow on its own. Not only does the tree compensate for carbon dioxide, but more importantly, the carbon-dioxide storage capacity of the bog contributes significantly to slowing climate change. In the meantime, an enormous amount of bog woodland has been created near Tribsees. This is also because a development rule was introduced stipulating that for every hectare of newly planted bog land, one house may be built in this area for the owner's use.

Scene change: We see a municipal official at their desk.

L: What does the Building Department think of this tree-planting campaign?
MO: The municipality has embraced the initiative of Ms. d. B. and, within the framework of an Article-19 procedure, has reformulated the land-use plan for the outskirts of the village. The principle of equality is no longer key, but rather the principle of appropriateness. "What is appropriate," you might ask—but that's always difficult to determine via legislation. So, we have set up a Reasonableness Jury, consisting of thirteen residents of Tribsees. This jury evaluates all plans and applications. Since 2028, any person who plants one hectare of bog woodland is permitted to build a house in this area. This hectare of moorland forest is overseen and maintained by the nature conservation authority: ten percent of this area, that is, 1,000 square meters, may be built upon for a home.

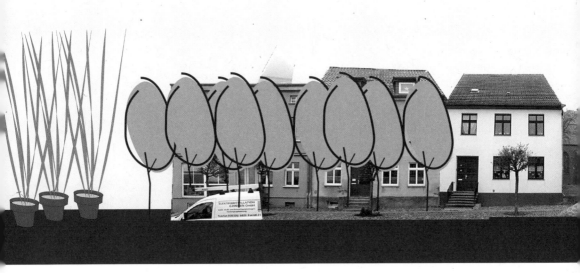

Karl-Marx-Straße

Horn MattonOffice & Herbert Winklehner
(Metal Workshop, University of Arts Linz)

Following the example of
the "complaint horn" from
Wittenburg, which unfortunately
no longer exists, we installed
a "compliment horn" in front
of the Tribsees town hall so
that residents could shout
their compliments through the
town. It was very popular, but
unfortunately late in the evening
in particular, so the horn was
quickly taped up again.

Tribsees/Linz

More Illuminated Advertising
space&designStrategies Students

Over the Christmas holiday season, these light works brought some rays of hope. They addressed vacancy, clichés, and possibilities for Tribsees based on the wishes of the residents.

Barth

Erica Speaks Silke Peters

My last train ride: changing trains in Velgast. The lady with the walker gets off. Changes trains. I have already seen her on the platform in Stralsund. She is traveling with a cherry tree in her basket. We plant shade trees, now as the first midsummer event. We do watering. We sweat. The chestnuts are still fresh and without the moth damage that was already predicted in Loitz. I walk barefoot across Devin at night. Summer. Twilight with hawthorn. I eat a few blossoms from the trees that stand on the shore. The water is just not cold anymore. My hair is already bleaching. Barth is still asleep. In the harbor, the boats sway in the bay. Someone has set up a couple of Slavic gods. A four-faced one. I take a few photos. The face of the church tower clock is blue. Witzlav had a castle. Bogislav, too. Vineta is disputed. But did it also sink? Pictures, as we know, are like a drink that does not quench our thirst, says W. J. T. Mitchell. The billboard, on which nothing has yet been glued again, is almost mute, weathered. On it the main sentences dissolve. Bardo is Polabian for a small elevation. It is the origin of the place name Barth, says Wikipedia and the authors' collective. This is the space between simple sentences. Starting somewhere, traveling somewhere. Sitting in the garden and looking. Ignite the thirst, in me, in the others? My car is silver, like the twilight over Devin, like the evaporating horizon line near

Dierhagen. Like the single seal on the beach. I have not taken a photo for you. The beach is still thinly populated by older tourists. I drive back and sleep in the garden shed. The roses open, smelling of roses? Ivy begins to climb up the old cherry tree. Light green. I am moved by the dusty footpaths on the shore. How they undulate, gently and endlessly. There is the place to jump once more into the river, as in a baptism. Diving. In Loitz, in Tribsees, or near Tressentin. There the rivers are the same. I built myself a canoe. From light wood and a hide. The imponderable other side but not reached. When I touch the rose bushes along the streets, they are still dripping wet from the thunderstorm that passed over the town this morning. The typewriter slowly remembers every single letter. To Dora Aßmann. She is registered. Who knows Dora Aßmann? Her registration data will surely fade away on the

brittle paper. Someone speaks: it's Erika. We run in a race. The morning star twinkles in the evening. It rains nails and beams on the small town. The low ceilings burst. Rubble. Charred beams. The river snorts the water lilies from its nostrils. Fairytale time. Once upon a time. A clearing. A hill by the

river. A castle. A safe place. Densely packed in their coops, chicks peep. I always enter the city through the mill gate. Through the milling district I enter. Circe. The many millers in the fairytales. The altars. The Cistercians find connection with running water. Nix or Nicholas are taken into service. Today, every place is assured. Raging floods. Outside the gates of the city lives the beautiful miller. The mill grinds in many voices. The hop runners empty the wish-mailbox. The chthonic, the uncontrollable proliferation has reached over the city walls. Moving aimlessly through the alleys. Like the fire dragon that is sometimes sighted at midnight. The inside and outside no longer suffice as a category. Mr. Himmelreich builds the scaffolding, the Jacob's ladders, the platforms along the collapsing facades. Silent mail. We search for the saying. Thomas lies over the gates, over the follies of the city.

Become passers-by, says Logion 42. The roses cascade onto the path, stunned by themselves, wheezing. There are emblematic empty trellises. There is a hunger for roses. There is a vineyard on the south wall. Fig trees cast shadows. We crawl through the detritus of days. Through things. They weather. In the summer air, everything is beautiful, glistening. The colors are saturated in a way. Tribsees is a bottomless barrel. A kind of wormhole to the other side.

Karl-Marx-Straße 80

Light Thief Vro Birkner

The cameras, made of welded steel, have a wide angle view and the long exposure time gives the images a certain romantic atmosphere that is well suited to the crumbling houses.

Slow Urban Planning

How can we redefine urban planning in our society? It should not be about maximum profits for project developers, or maximum power for politicians, or maximum freedom for individuals. The goal should be the creation of concrete freedoms for society. There is no need for a blueprint for a new future. We can continue to use our land-use planning procedures at the regional level and try to formulate approaches and thought-provoking ideas for slow urban planning.

Somehow, the Ministry for Housing, Urban Development, and Building should prescribe how people are to live and draw up a set of rules that will prevent undesirable developments while creating desirable opportunities—after all, the light and fresh air thing worked out pretty well back then. But let's be concrete about this: if we want to improve the carbon footprint, for example, we could stipulate that every person who wants to build a house in Tribsees must plant a tree on the property and care for it; or even an entire forest, with a clearing where a small house can then be built. Since, as Minister Geywitz also says, we should reduce our consumption of meat from large farms and discourage factory farming, we could mandate that each person who wants to build a house in Tribsees should provide space for five happy chickens and a rooster, or for two equally happy free-range pigs. (Do not get me wrong. It's not about compliance with European laws and requirements for free-range husbandry in the service of economic goals, but about the welfare of the animals.) In order to reduce fossil energy consumption and provide more sustainable energy, it would be mandatory to build a wind turbine on the property, perhaps even one that you could live in. But this will only be approved if the town is also connected to the power supply. Halving the space requirement from fifty to twenty-five square meters, as the minister proposes, is not necessary in the countryside, however, which is precisely where the surplus of space should be celebrated.

That may sound ideological and extreme at first. But in Saarlouis, for example, the city gave away as many as three trees to interested residents in the fall of 2022 and even financed their professional planting. In return, the property owners agreed to water their trees regularly, especially in the first few years, and to permanently maintain them.[1] Obviously, then, it is possible to organize the handing out of trees and that is a first step. Making tree planting compulsory is not easy, that's perfectly clear, but within

---

1 See Joachim Göres, "Bäume zu verschenken," *Süddeutsche Zeitung,* September 3–4, 2022, p. 42.

a heterotopic experiment it could be a good place to start.

Refuge T. Tribsees

Tribsees could be developed as a kind of refuge, a heterotopian island where you could live an easy-going life within the city walls, behind the towers, undisturbed by the neoliberal rat race and free of debt. Refuge T. Tribsees, loosely based on the work of Arne Næss.[2]

Precisely because there are so many vacant sites in Tribsees, you could make a kind of tabula rasa. Not in the sense of clearing out the entire town center to build a new shopping center following a modernist blueprint, but rather, to establish a more morally grounded tabula rasa that would allow for the emergence of a place within the city walls where global problems are eradicated at the local level.

Hypermodernity

The slow urban planning in Tribsees would be a kind of parallel urbanism, an exploration carried out within the hypermodernity of small-town life, a search for a more relaxed and responsible way of life, for a town in which you could live in an atmosphere where time, space, and action were still synchronized. This would ensure the essential qualities for living. This does not mean lapsing into nostalgic traditionalism, but rather exploring what was good in the past and harnessing that for today's global world. What is meant here is not the creation of a technological utopia. Rather, our approach is based on hypermodernist research that shows what elements from history can be applied to our society today and combined with new technologies. Potential solutions should be located within the context of regional authenticity: carbon neutral, sustainable energy production; clean water supply; recyclable materials; all fair trade, all organic, no products from slave or child labor. These are the goals we would like to achieve through slow urban planning.

Broad Welfare

Slow urban planning could be based on the broad welfare model.[3] This involves a fruitful symbiosis between material well-being, egalitarian opportunities for all, and good living conditions, today and

2   Loosely based on deep ecologist Arne Næss, "Ecosophy T," in *Ecology, Community and Lifestyle*, Cambridge: Cambridge University Press, 1989.

3   MattonOffice for OMA/AMO 2010, see Ton Matton: "Produktion von Wohlbefinden. Ein träger Entwicklungsplan für die Côte d'Azur," in Ton Matton: *Zweifel. Performative Stadtplanung in 13 Vorträgen*, Berlin: Jovis, 2019, pp. 52–61.

in the future. This leads to greater well-being for society. In a broad welfare model, for example, all factors that are important in the production and consumption of a product are taken into account, such as energy requirements, waste recycling, pollutant emissions, transportation, etc., but also social aspects such as fair wages, healthy working conditions, opportunities for individual development, and so on. Paretian welfare theory is based upon reproducible goods and consumption; it does not consider non-reproducible goods such as art, landscape, and clean air. A comprehensive, broader welfare theory takes all of these into account and thus moves closer to Latourian territory.[4] On an urban scale, implementing this type of moral economy is a complex matter. But it is precisely this moral economy that can attract people and businesses who want to demonstrate their responsible lifestyles.

Survival Pack

In his book, *The Man Without Qualities*, Robert Musil states: "But if there is such a thing as a sense of reality— and no one will doubt that it has its raison d'être—then there must also be something that one can call a sense of possibility. ... So the sense of possibility might be defined outright as the capacity to think how everything could 'just as easily' be, and to attach no more importance to what is than to what is not."[5] Urban planners and politicians with a sense of reality often rely on the modernist belief that technology can save the world. But it is not only shrinking regions that show that this approach no longer works. We are consuming more than our one earth allows; on May 4, 2022, Germany had already used up its ecological resources for that year. We cannot simply carry on as before; with the knowledge available to us today that would be criminal. The nationwide information campaign on self-help in the event of a disaster prepared by the German Federal Office of Civil Protection and Disaster Assistance (BBK)—"How to Prepare for Disasters"—focuses on

4   See Arnold Heertje, *Echte economie. Een verhandeling over schaarste en welvaart en over het geloof in leermeesters en lernen,* Nijmegen: Valkhof Pers, 2006.

5   Robert Musil, *The Man Without Qualities,* volume 1, New York: Vintage International, 1996, p. 16. [German original edition: *Der Mann ohne Eigenschaften,* Berlin: Rowohlt, 1930–1934].

individual preparedness. The aim of the campaign is to sensitize the population to the issues of self-protection and self-help to raise risk awareness and to contribute to greater resilience among the population through concrete precautionary and behavioral recommendations. This was a societal mission seventy years ago as part of the capitalist Rhineland Model, tailored to meet political objectives. In today's neoliberal society, we seem to be left to our own devices. This is precisely where slow urban planning picks up.

Tribsees/Linz

Yet More Illuminated Advertising
space&designStrategies Students

The few hours of sunshine in northern Europe were barely enough (if at all) to allow the Linz students' solar-powered illuminated objects to shine.

Courtyard High-Rise

09/13/2048 Post by the successful influencer L.

 196K   8.557   98.922

... in which a project developer (PD) talks about a new form of housing in Tribsees.

We see the camera following the project developer on a walk through Tribsees.

PD: I still remember learning during my studies in the nineteen-seventies that money always came first. Housing didn't have to be as inexpensive as possible, as was the case before, when even liberals still had a social agenda; at that point, the most important thing was to make a lot of profit. Fortunately, this has changed, and, as we have found here in Tribsees, good housing definitely contributes to a more fulfilled life. So, we developed this high-rise, where several family homes of the popular EW58 type from the former GDR are stacked on top of each other. This is a rural version of the urban high-rise with small green balconies. Here, not only the houses are stacked, but the entire property, including the garden and courtyard. The idea comes from an early twentieth-century illustration by a certain Mr. Walker, published in an American newspaper. People garden on their own floor and are self-sufficient. What was good in the past—small-scale, environmentally friendly, sustainable—is here integrated into a contemporary building form. After years of criticizing neoliberalism, it is gratifying that the social dimension is

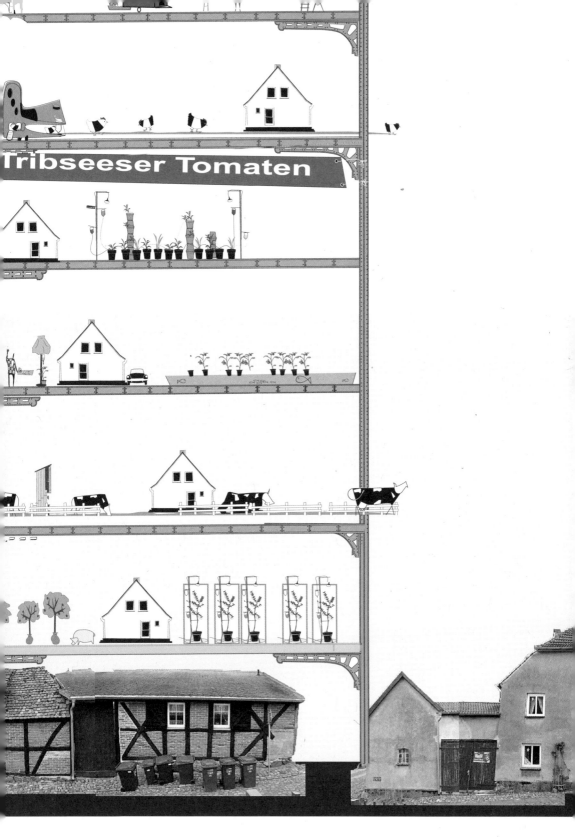

Tribseeser Tomaten

once again coming to the fore. In this respect, Tribsees is now a pioneer as well as a model project for many communities.

L: Do you wish the GDR would come back?

PD: Never, no. But the fact that you can build your own house, not all at once with a lot of debt to the bank, but just step by step, building with your own hands—that's enormously satisfying. Look, there, on the fourth floor, tomatoes are grown. And the waste is sent to the fish farm on the third floor, just below. This is the aquaponics method, in other words. On the sixth floor, there are pigs. They eat all the leftovers from the neighbors on the other floors. Fresh eggs are available on the fifth floor, where happy chickens scratch around, with a magnificent view over the small town. The houses are largely self-sufficient. Electricity comes from the local wind farm, water is recycled, and waste is reused.

The owner of the cows has now also started making fresh cheese. If you are lucky, she will treat you to an excellent cup of coffee, with real milk, not the excessively sweet oat drink that is served everywhere in the big cities.

Karl-Marx-Straße 69

Dance House Isabel Kufner

Influenced by protective measures
against the coronavirus, Isabel Kufner
created this solo dance house in the
dilapidated passageway of this vacant
building.

Karl-Marx-Straße 69

Land Route Chaz Gervais

Across the country, from
Rostock to Stralsund, from
Schwerin to Greifswald,
Chaz Gervais rode his bike
and distributed stickers
advertising the routes.
All his bicycle routes led
through Tribsees—in the
hope of attracting enough
cyclists to Tribsees who
would then stop at the
newly opened café and in
this way help to keep it
open.

University of Arts Linz

Tribsees House in Linz space&designStrategies Symposium
with Christopher Dell, Rianne Makkink, & Xian Zheng

In the general spirit of demolition, the importance of improvisation and thinking in terms of possibilities was debated, not only for a small town like Tribsees, but also for teaching at an art university. Behind a lectern made

of Tribsees bricks, Ton Matton gave his exit speech from the window of the space&designStrategies rooms of the University of Arts Linz. Afterwards, the archive from seven years of classes was shredded and blown into the courtyard with a confetti cannon.

Tribsees Senior Citizens Residence

04/11/2062 Post by the successful influencer L.

... in which a resident (ST) tells about her life in the Tribsees Senior Citizens Residence.

We see ST sitting at the breakfast table in the restaurant, where she is eating a country breakfast with scrambled eggs and homemade jam, accompanied by a small glass of Rotkäppchen sparkling wine.

L: That looks good! Do you eat here every day?
ST: Always on Wednesdays and Fridays. There are three other dining rooms that I go to, they're part of the residence as well. The food tastes really good.

Everything you order here comes from Tribsees. Not only the jam and the eggs, but even the dishes come from Tribsees; we have a long pottery tradition. You see the little red spots? Those are made from the old, crushed bricks from houses that collapsed back then.
L: That means you eat off of your old houses?
ST: Ha ha, yes, you could say that. At that time, artists and the pottery association worked together to develop their own dishware, which was made from the bricks that had become waste material. This became a success story. Many of the residents at that time made

pottery for the love of it, and so, piece by piece, they used up the old broken bricks. And because a senior citizens residence was developed in the town, all the old residents could stay here and pass on their knowledge of pottery production to the coming generations.
L: Do many people from back then still live here?
ST: Yes, indeed. Because quite a few of the empty houses scattered around the town center back then, at least thirty-five of them, were developed into senior residences, making it possible to stay here even in old age. It's nice not to have to live amidst the hustle and bustle of the big city just because there's a hospital there. There are various dining rooms, a cinema, a billiard café, and of course, well-maintained housing. Everything is in the immediate vicinity. You could say it's like a nursing home but spread out over the entire town center. Medical care, nursing services, recreational programs, and shopping are all available. I live as independently as I've always wanted to, but I can still get the care I need, tailored to my needs ... and every now and then a glass of sparkling wine at breakfast. What a wonderful way to live. Cheers!

Senior residence restaurant

Residence 12

Residence 3

Nordmauerstraße

Wellness in Hotel Tribsees MattonOffice

You could use the solar shower right on the riverbank—in the DIY spa of the Grand Hotel Tribsees. With water from the Trebel, heated by the sun (when it shone) or even just cold.

Wasserwanderrastplatz (Waterside Rest Area)

Ich kann deine Zukunft sehen! Bernadette La Hengst

Ich hab' nichts in Berlin verloren, mein Herz hängt zwischen deinen Toren, / Du bist mein Heim und spätes Glück, die Liebe auf den zweiten Blick. / In den Freiluftgalerien / Ist Platz für deine Utopien, das Trebel Café gibt es schon, für alle die hier gerne wohn'!

Tribsees, Tribsees, ich kann deine Zukunft sehen, / Bald wirst, bald wirst du nicht mehr so leer rumstehen, denn / Tribsees, Tribsees, bevor du vom Wind verwehst, / Halte ich dich fest, denn ich kann deine Zukunft sehen: Tribsees!

Ein Salsa Kurs mit Tangotanz, / Weltoffenheit und Eleganz, / Ein Büchercafé in der Stadt, / Mit Lesungen, auch mal auf Platt, / Repair Cafés für jung und alt, / Mit Omas Kräutern aus dem Wald, / Wir tauschen Handarbeiten aus, / Und Fensterhäkeln jedes Haus.

Tribsees, Tribsees, ich kann deine Zukunft sehen ...

Leere Häuser klein und groß, sind bald nicht mehr seelenlos, / Familien mit Kind und Hund, komm'n aus Rostock und Stralsund, / Wir wollen Nachbarn, die hier leben und nicht nur ihr Geld anlegen, / Wir sind Tribsees' Kapital und unsre Zukunft ist schon da: / Ich kann sie sehen ... sehen ... Ich kann sie sehen ... sehen ... / Ich kann sie sehen ... sehen ... Ich kann sie sehen ... Tribsees!

(Für die Dörfer ringsherum, werden wir zum Stadtzentrum, / Restaurants und Ateliers, und ein Kinderparadies, / Eine Brücke übers Moor, kommt und singt mit uns im Chor):

Tribsees, Tribsees, ich kann deine Zukunft sehen, / Bald wirst, bald wirst du nicht mehr so leer rumstehen, denn / Tribsees, Tribsees, bevor du vom Wind verwehst, / Halte ich dich fest, denn ich kann deine Zukunft sehen: Tribsees!

Inside the theater built from straw bales by farmer Rohlfing, Bernadette La Hengst sang the hit song "Ich kann deine Zukunft sehen!" (I can see your future!) with the Tribsees Future Choir.

Nordmauerstraße

Hotel Tribsees Bar Jey Roesner

The garden of the former Kiek In (Peep In) bar became the bar and breakfast room of the Grand Hotel Tribsees. Run by Jey Roesner, there was something to eat and drink in a relaxed atmosphere at any time of the day.

Tribsees/Linz

And Even More Illuminated Advertising
space&designStrategies Students

Herzliche Einladung zur
TRIBSEESER CENTENNIALE
24.Juni bis 29. August 2021
ZWISCHEN DEN TOREN
mit lokalen und internationalen KünstlerInnen,
Raum-und DesignStrategInnen,
allen Gästen und den Tribseeser BürgerInnen

HERZLICHE EINLADUNG ZUR
FINISSAGE
DER TRIBSEESER CENTENNIALE
26.AUGUST BIS 28.AUGUST
internationalen KünstlerInnen, Raum-und Design
allen Gästen und den Tribseeser BürgerInnen

Tribseeser Chor
mit Bernadette LaHengst
Konzert am 28.August 18:00
am Wasserwanderrastplatz

Bulli-Tour durch MV
Liedermacherin Barbara Thalheim
und Mathias Greffrath
„In welcher Gesellschaft wollen wir leben?
Reden wir drüber."

VERNISSAGE
am 24. Juni ab 17:00
mit
Minister Pegel &
olländische Botschaft (eingeladen)
und
Bürgermeister & Professor
und
KünstlerInnen & StudentInnen
und
Improvisations-Jazz-Musiker
ristopher Dell & Theo Jürgensmann

MIDISSAGE
22.Juli bis 25.Juli
mit
Campingtafel
am 24. Juli 15:00
mit dem Motorsportverein Touristik Tribsees
Wohnmobilie sind Willkommen!
und
Tango zum Vollmond
am 24. Juli 20:00
mit den Tangogruppen der Region
Tänzer herbeispaziert!
und
Freilichtkino
am 23.Juli 22:00
mit Tribsees lädt zu Tisch
Stühle, Popcorn und Getränke bitte selbst mitbringen!

Kaffeetafel
mit dem Tribseeser Frauenverein
am 28. August 14:00
Zwischen den Toren

Grafittikunst zum selber machen
26. bis 28. August Zwischen den Toren
Farbe und Fläche werden gestellt
Preisverleihung mit Verwirklichung

Ute Gallmeister
mit dem Archäologischen Museum
Karl-Marx-Straße 09

Susanne Gabler
REPARATUREN AM HAUS
Knochenhauerstraße 23, 24

KINO
am 23.Juni
ab Sonnenuntergang

Knochenhauerstraße

Moving House MattonOffice: Ton, Sofie, Paulus, Chaz, Yue & Anna

If students can't go to Tribsees, then we'll bring Tribsees to Linz: this was the statement that started the idea of the moving house. In fact, a dilapidated house was transported to Linz by truck. Ton had already relocated the EW58 GDR house from Mecklenburg-Vorpommern to Almere in 2008 and so had already gained some experience with this kind of relocation. Hundreds of bricks, broken windows, gutters, power cables, and wooden beams, all packed on pallets, were a great worry for the superintendent who was concerned about the structural stability of the university building. In the end, everything worked out wonderfully and the students who couldn't make it to Tribsees were able to use these materials to create their own semester projects.

Knochenhauerstraße

Narrative Thread Susanne Gabler with Marlene Adam, Brigitte Blodow, Sonja Gruse, Marianne Freuer, Rita Monka, Regina Quade, Sigrid Ratz & Helga Rudolph

In this small town on the Trebel River, the large project "Making Tribsees's Future" has been running for a year. As part of this project, much has already happened in Tribsees, including my project HOME REPAIRS. To do this, I went to Tribsees as an artist, let the place have an effect on me, and talked to the people of Tribsees. Up to seventy houses are in ruins, in an otherwise well (?) preserved urban structure. The past of the place, which can be read from this, is a treasure and a torment at the same time. I find beauty in the midst of these structures, but I ask myself why? Because I recognize old times, because I see some things from my own early days, and because I understand many things here. The

tranquility and lucidity of this forgotten town is transferred onto me and I find my focus. The vacancy is heartbreaking, the ruins are attractive. It is the many small structures that lure me close to the facades, doors, and windows. What does Tribsees need? Repaired houses? I love to do repairs. However, so far, I have only one technique for this: I sew. Then I will sew a house! This was a very obvious idea, because I found the most beautiful crack in Tribsees. I will sew it up, as beautifully as you can sew a crack in a house. Golden fastenings, golden nails, with sewing thread that must be delicate and of a pretty color. A color that suits Tribsees and my feelings in this place—dusty rose. Now I'm sewing a house. Sewing a tear in

the house like a wound on the body. Therein lies all my compassion as well as my complete respect for Tribsees, its buildings, and the people there. Perhaps the women felt that. Three of them—Siegried, Gitti, and Marlene— met with me and we decided to do the repairs together. On a walk, we found two very suitable houses that were crumbling together—"held together by a common wall," as the former owner explained to me. Siegried, Marlene, and Gitti belong to the Tribsees Women's Association and I was invited two weeks later to their association rooms. On that day, fifteen women now sat across from me and eight of them took several rolls of my dusty rose crochet yarn. We discussed my concept: the women display their needlework art in all its facets. To reveal the aesthetics of the infinite arrangements and combinations of stitches, chain stitches, and treble stitches, it only

takes one material, in one color. With my dusty rose yarn, we all agreed. Women's handicrafts are a tradition among them. This tradition is very valuable. Putting this valuable thing on the crumbling houses highlights the value of these buildings and the urban structure. Helga weaves bricks because they are rotten in some corners. Now the house is crocheted, sewn, and woven in dusty rose. In an interview, Gitte emphasized this with a wagging index finger: "We are not glaziers. We are crocheters and weavers." I like working with the women. They bring hot coffee, a table, homemade cakes, and cushioned chairs. We sit together, they crochet, and I sew. In the process, they show me how to twist the delicate yarn and how to crochet a simple chain stitch. Of course, I learn the latest gossip as well as many interesting facts about Tribsees. We connect with each other in a direct, tactile sense,

I connect with Tribsees, the traditions of Tribsees women connect with their town, and the past connects with the future. I hope that everyone will recognize the value of this in our REPAIRS.

Karl-Marx-Straße

From Here to "Here" Yue Hu

The project "From Here to 'Here'—Interaction of Artistic Practice and Society" deals with the increasing divide between social groups. This gap increases the alienation between people, between people and places, and between people and society as a whole—and as a result also affects the creativity of artists, who increasingly lose sight of how their artistic practice can play a role in overcoming social problems.

As part of her PhD work, Yue Hu spent a few weeks in Tribsees shooting a short film. Some stills from the film have been included in this publication. You can see how the word "Here," which she wrote on the ground with water and a brush, slowly evaporates.

She is referring to the Chinese tradition of painting propagandistic slogans on walls. She made similar works in Dong Men Kou, a village in China, as well as in Vienna and Shanghai, among other places.

Südmauerstraße

Slow Development Plans

What could emerge from this is a model in which local residents improvise and try to build responsible lives. This is an evolutionary process where growth draws upon the historical emergence of small towns, step by step. Of course, the impact in each place will be different—sometimes it will be a great success, and sometimes a flop. These kinds of extremes are precisely the goal of slow urban planning, as a counterbalance to the secure mediocrity of comfortable suburbs. Whether it's a matter of food, energy supply, water management, health care, work, or housing, through slow urban planning in Tribsees, residents can find their own individual position in order to shape alternative answers to these topics, based on their own desires and ideas. The goal is to generate diversity within the range of activities being offered. This does not necessarily have to remain on a small scale, but nevertheless must evolve bit by bit through a local process.

Reasonableness

With the help of slow urban planning, the fundamental ideal of equality changes into a basic concept of individual, local possibilities and responsibilities. The concern that what is approved must be valid for all is based on a fair distribution for the average person, without extremes, without disruption. In slow urban planning, the principle of reasonableness is the goal. A democratic jury should assess how building applications contribute to the immediate environment, in both negative and positive ways. Representatives of the local government as well as residents who are directly affected should have a seat on the reasonableness jury. They will judge the submitted proposals. Individual building projects are only to be approved if the applicant submits a plan that meets the political goals and associated requirements. These may vary according to the plot of land but must always be based on a broad welfare economy. It is not a matter of questioning the right to equality. Rather, the aim is to find site-specific, local, individual, tailor-made answers to all of today's global problems, as appropriate to the territory.

This (re)interpretation of the urban planning profession is given new impetus, perhaps even a new sense of pride, by a proposal such as this. With their knowledge of urban development, urban planners can once again take on the role of (social) advisors to policymakers rather than executors. In the end, a town is not only about buildings and streets, but also about people.

Territory

The existing rules and regulations have grown over the last centuries and are based on the local building site as a territory, with modernist considerations such as housing, work, mobility, recreation, and the accessibility of each site and the distances between them. But our territory has expanded enormously. Providing clean water from a building site is no longer just a question of a water pipe with a meter. The question is expanding: how clean is the groundwater? Thus, groundwater contamination by nitrates from agriculture becomes a part of the building site—even if it is not located directly in this agricultural area. Clean air also belongs to the plot of land—and with it comes the carbon-dioxide debate. Weekly garbage collection is not only about waste separation—the plastic in the ocean is also part of this globalized territorial thinking, as is our entire consumer behavior. In *Down to Earth: Politics in the New Climatic Regime*, Bruno Latour describes how all scientific, economic, and political disciplines rely on their own arguments about sustainability.[1] Individual disciplines set rules to solve a particular problem without taking a broader view. But the globalization of the world also brings responsibilities; it is not only about the benefits of the world market, but also about the inclusion of all global territory, the habitability of the Earth.

Our modernist thinking must end, and a broader basis established on which to define and plan our society, in an interdisciplinary manner, based on welfare distribution and production. As Latour claims, this is an ecologization by which aspects from a wide variety of truths, such as politics, science, religion, and fiction, are brought together. In so doing, urban planning should take up a more anthropological position.

Influencer

Slow urban planning could produce new rules from this kind of more holistic approach. Perhaps it is up to the successful influencer L., who as a teenager witnessed the whole process in Tribsees—lived it, and even helped create it—to embrace a slow urban planning approach in the future as mayor of Tribsees and to turn the town into a center for the production of well-being. The initially limited area of Tribsees would allow for a pragmatic approach. Slow urban planning encourages new ways of sustainable and fair development. This example, considered in its entirety, leads to rule proposals (see page 147), which Mayor L. together with the Reasonableness Jury would discuss, modify, add to, and adopt until, in turn, new insights, adjustments, and changes were required.

1   See Bruno Latour, *Down to Earth: Politics in the New Climatic Regime,* Cambridge: Polity Press, 2018 [French original edition: *Où atterrir? Comment s'orienter en politique,* Paris: Éditions La Découverte, 2017].

World Ranking of Climate-Friendly Cities

In addition, by establishing this type of moral objective, Tribsees could move up in the world ranking of climate-friendly cities. To become the most "eco" place in the world, all you have to do is find that one issue related to "eco" that hasn't been covered yet, or adopt a topic that has already been covered and become a leader in the field: just as Copenhagen is the capital of bicycles and Masdar is the solar energy capital, and just as Curitiba is the public transportation champion, Tribsees will become the moral heterotopia. In the business of professional politics, this is simply a matter of definition and creative calculation (just as there are three world-leading waterfalls—the highest, the widest, the one with the most water). And it is just smart to return to Burnham: "Make no little plans. Make big plans."

§127
Whoever wants to build in Tribsees should eat organic products.

§85
Every house needs a compost heap.

§53
On each plot happy pigs may be raised in free-range and organic conditions.

§29
Within the city walls, only fair trade and organic food may be consumed.

§45
Plastic is only allowed if a plastic worm farm, where the worm denizens break down and eat the plastic, is incorporated in the construction.

§7
Construction is allowed if the building can produce more energy than it consumes over the course of a year.

§7.3
The energy used in construction is expected to be offset within ten years.

§17
Wastewater should be treated on the property and may only be removed if this will improve groundwater quality.

§74
Whoever wants to pass through the city walls should wear fair trade clothes.

§96
The architect of the building is not allowed to wear black clothes, whose dye pollutes the rivers.

§86
Every new building should contribute to cleaning the air.

§59
Habitats for a variety of animal species should be created on each plot.

§61
Construction outside the city walls is only permitted if ninety percent of the garden is renaturalized as bog woodland.

§57
If you want to drive an electric car, then you must plant one tree per year and care for it yourself; a gasoline or diesel car requires ten trees for every 10,000 kilometers driven.

Karl-Marx-Straße 9

Archaeological Museum Ute Gallmeister

Ute Gallmeister went on a search for vestiges of the past together with a few people from Tribsees. Many details were captured using relief printing techniques and displayed in the Archaeological Museum.

Linz/Wendorf/Tribsees

McTrebelBurger Peiyan Zhang

Peiyan Zhang conjured up this McTrebel-Burger from old bricks, using wallpaper as lettuce and electricity cables as onions. This was received with such enthusiasm that Peiyan used his term project to produce an edible version as well—a huge success with the people of Tribsees!

Regional Land Use Development

Experiment Tanja Blankenburg

In the course of developing the 2016 state regional development program, we introduced a new spatial category in Mecklenburg-Vorpommern, the "Rural Design Areas." By this means, we wanted to identify regions in the state that are particularly weak in terms of infrastructure and subsequently support their development through special measures. To this end, a fund was set up for projects aimed at meeting the special challenges facing these regions. An interministerial working group chaired by the head of the State Chancellery decided how the funds were to be used, but technical support was primarily provided by a state development team in the then-Ministry of Energy, Infrastructure,

and Digitalization headed by Hermann Brinkmann, of which Claudia Meier and I were members. In addition, interdisciplinary and interdepartmental coordination was carried out by the Dialog Working Group, whose dedicated colleagues from the other ministries supported and assisted in the work. What was special about our approach was that we were allowed to deliberately go off the beaten path. The naming of this spatial category was not intended to be mere window dressing, as some suggested. The term "design" was meant programmatically, in the sense of a creative, innovative, formative, experimental approach. It is a fact of everyday administrative life that not all ideas can always be

realized in the way that is sometimes desired. The use of public funds is regulated by guidelines, ordinances, and laws. Funding programs pursue particular goals and require clearly defined prerequisites, the logic of which may not be compatible with some projects. That is why we have designed the fund for the Rural Design Areas in such a way that we can also finance projects that would have been difficult to support through other funding instruments.

This flexibility made this experiment possible, the result of which can be found in the pages of this publication. I think it was worth it. The work of Ton Matton and his collaborator Sofie Wagner has changed the way Tribsees residents look at their town—perhaps by allowing them to discover new potentials and possibilities there, or simply giving them a new perspective. Together with contributors from

elsewhere, they have enriched the city through their artistic activities and have attracted significant media attention. Thus, many outsiders will also have discovered the charm of the little town. I hope that the residents of the town, as well as people from outside, have been encouraged to invest in the future of this place—whether with ideas or money—while preserving its unique character. May we continue to eat, sing, dance, and celebrate together on the streets of the town, as we did during the months of this successful experiment. Making Tribsees's Future!

Tribsees/Linz

The Gold of Tribsees MattonOffice & Pedram Feizbakhsh

Tribsees Senior Residency

Tribsees Cheese Market

Vacancy seen as a treasure: Pedram sketched out a wide variety of future scenarios for Tribsees.

Special thanks go to

Mr. Zentner and the **Bauhof** for their welcome and much needed support; the **Bauunternehmen Wiese**—not only for opening doors; **DÖRING Bauschuttaufbereitung & Abbruch** for all kinds of construction debris; the **Regionale Schule mit Grundschule Recknitz-Trebeltal** for the many creative tiles made by their students; **Simone Karl** for the unique store window; the **Strukturförderverein Trebeltal Stremlow** and **Ms. Schröder** for their ever-ready helping hands and the collaborative construction work in the dilapidated department store; **Torsten Flöttmann** for everything—and for luring us to the baroque village of Nehringen; the **Vogelparkregion Recknitztal Tourism Association** for the great networking; the **Tranquillo Handelsgesellschaft**—especially **Raoul Scheimeister**—for golden liquids; **Uwe Bobsin** for the stimulating discussions; **Wolfgang Stenzel** for his incredible knowledge of Tribsees; the students from the **space&designStrategies course at the University of Arts Linz** for their exciting strategies and many fabulous projects; **Bipin Rao** and **Jonathan Holstein** for providing beautiful lighting and music until the early morning hours; **Florian Schulz** for the event technology; **Thomas Reich and His Band** for great concerts; **Muzet Royal** for a thousand tangos, at least; **Susanne Gabler** for her beautiful crocheted works; **Ute Gallmeister** for making art under high pressure; the **Alter Pfarrhof Elmenhorst**

for delicious baked goods; **Anna-Lena Auth** for organizational support and her bar skills; **Silke Peters** for Erica; **Weiqi Wang** for ideas for the future in stone and clay; **Jey Roesner** for her ever pleasant support; **Gertraud Kliment** for her commitment; **Herbert Winklehner** for the steely horn; the **Lighting Designers of the Hochschule Wismar** for many bright ideas; **Michael Kockot** for film and photography; the **Filmklub Güstrow** for the revival of the Tribsees open-air cinema; **Martha** and **Beate** from **morgen.** for their very convincing social design; **Marco** and **Jan** from **Hirn und Wanst** for many exciting film fragments; **Florian Gwinner** for the balcony scene; **Hermann Brinkmann** (†) and **Tanja Blankenburg** for having the courage to tackle this project and for their constant support; **Christian Pegel** for many unexpected, helpful visits; **Bernhard Zieris** for not despairing in all the many weird moments; **Steffi Timm** for her trust and her always energized good mood; **Lukas Schrader** for culinary cooperation—day and night; **Lutz Bornhöft** for being Lutz and for the delicious nourishment; **Nicole Wenzel** for the best cheese in Mecklenburg-Vorpommern; the **Youth Club** for its total commitment to Tribsees's future; **Annette Schmid** for everything—and especially to the entire **Gärtnerei Schmid** for their efforts; the **Arbeitslosentreff** together with **Ms. Senft** for coffee pots and dishes; the **Wasserwanderrastplatz** and

Mr. **Beyer** for accommodation, showers, and bratwurst; the **Trebel Pottery** and **Hilde Zinke** for recycling the pulverized bricks; **Julia Kaiser** for the urban-rural ceramic exchange; **Krautkopf** for the aesthetic-culinary design of the church; **Nina Janoschka** for being "Super-Nina"; the **Women's Association** and **Ms. Quade**, **Ms. Blodow**, and **Ms. Teetz** for their support ... as well as the ironing party; **Jürgen Groth** for his advisory support; the **Kaffeeklappe** for the delicious nourishment in the restaurant; the **Fire Department Band** and **Mr. Krüger** for the musical revival; **Blütenzauber Tribsees** for their support in selling Tribsees-to-Table tickets; the **Café Wunder Bar** (Bad Sülze) for helping to sell Tribsees-to-Table tickets; **Demokratie leben!** for their financial support; **Bernadette La Hengst** for the great Tribsees anthem; the **Church Choir** and **Ms. Schulze** for the beautiful singing; the **Tribsees Volunteer Fire Brigade** and **Mr. Horn** as well as the **Youth Fire Brigade** and **Ms. Wernicke** for many illuminating operations; **Regio-Ring Richtenberger See** for opening up and expanding the network; **Spiritus Rex** for high-quality regional delicacies; **Café Tribsees** and **Ms. Biederhorn** together with the **Mittag family** for many delicious cakes; the **Motorsports Club** along with **Ms. Stoll** and **Mr. Voigt** for even more delicious cakes; the **Church Youth** and **Ms. Teske** for building the new town (give me water, I'll stir the lime); **EDEKA Dumnick** for helping to sell Tribsees-to-Table tickets; **fritz-kulturgüter** for quenching guests' thirst; **Gutshaus Landsdorf** for local culinary expertise; **Arbeitskreis Asyl** and **Mr. Kaufmann** for international engagement and translation; **GuGs Gebäude- und Grundstücksservice** together with **Mr. Bohla** for working at great heights; **Pastor Detlef Huckfeldt** for opening doors and providing blessed support; the **Ministry of the Interior, Building, and Digitalization Mecklenburg-Vorpommern** for the generous support; the **Kramer family** for reliable onsite assistance; **Mr. Levandowski** for many (emotional) work assignments; **Ms. Meyer** from Landsdorf for her neighborly engagement; town chronicler **Siegfried Casper** for a great many anecdotes; storyteller **Mr. Lemke** for exciting tales; neighbor **Mr. Niedorff** for a beer or two on his bench; the **Schnelles Grünzeug** nursery for the fun of experimenting and sharing knowledge; **Rats-Apotheke Tribsees** for helping to sell Tribsees-to-Table tickets; the **Ratsherrn Brewery** for hoppy support; **Gärtnerei Weber** for greening the rock garden; **Pilzhof Wittenhagen** for fungal delicacies; **Mr. Rohlfing** the farmer for a straw-bale theater; **Mr. Seget** from **Tribsees train station** for shower tokens and backstage wood; **Lina Meier** for everything!; **Black Delight Kaffee** for delicious black gold; **Ms. Kuhn** for the beautiful accommodation; **all empty house owners, would-be house owners, heirs**, and **those not contacted** for enabling us to think in terms of possibilities!; **Mr. Hävernick** for permission to use Karl-Marx-Straße 50; **Mr. Grave** for permission to use Karl-Marx-Straße 48; **Christopher Dell** and **Theo Jörgensmann** for improvised jazz; **Sofie Wagner** for the super social project management, once again; **Ton Matton** for yet more exciting performative urban planning

© 2023 by jovis Verlag GmbH
Texts by kind permission of the
authors.
Pictures by kind permission of
the photographers/holders of the
picture rights.

Cover image: MattonOffice: Ton
Matton, Sophie Kleppin
Translation: Dr. David Haney
Copy-editing: Christen Jamar
Design: MattonOffice: Ton Matton,
Sophie Kleppin
Lithography: Bild1Druck
Printed in the European Union

Bibliographic information published
by the Deutsche Nationalbibliothek:
The Deutsche Nationalbibliothek
lists this publication in the Deutsche
Nationalbibliografie; detailed bibliographic data are available on the
Internet at http://dnb.d-nb.de.

jovis Verlag GmbH
Lützowstraße 33
10785 Berlin

www.jovis.de

jovis books are available worldwide in
select bookstores. Please contact your
nearest bookseller or visit www.jovis.de
for information concerning your local
distribution.

ISBN 978-3-86859-769-1